Do I Need To Slap You?

How To Avoid Stupid Relationship Mistakes

Michele Hickford

Design by Viro S
Photo by vimkrugerphotography.com

Many thanks to the Editors:

Jules, Fran, Adali, Jeannie, Judie, Julie, Young, Ruby, Lori, Linda, Kim, Laurel, Phyllis, Marianne, Tracy, Kelly, Tom, and especially Karen for making me get off my butt.

But most of all, thanks to John McGran for opening the door.

 INTRODUCTION

Thank goodness you're reading this book. I certainly hope you actually bought it, but what the heck, at least you're reading it. That's a start.

Now I don't want you to take this personally, but...well, you know what? Actually I DO want you to take this personally. Very personally. I want you to know I wrote this just for you.

Because I'm the one who has to listen to all your endless hashing and rehashing of romantic problems. Not that I don't find it entertaining...because I do – but I just think you're making things waaaaaaay too difficult and complicated or spending waaaaaaay too much time in the wrong relationship.

The way I look at it is relationships take effort, but they shouldn't be hard work. And all too often I hear you going through an awful lot of hard work for not very much in return.

So I put together this compilation of things I think you should know about relationships. What makes me an expert? Well, I've been around the block a few times, and I've heard from hundreds of people all around the globe who amazingly suffer from the same problems you do and quite possibly need a slap upside the head to knock some sense into them too.

I want you to have a better life. I want you to fulfill your potential and be healthier and happier in your relationships and have perfect hair and a twinkle in your eye and a little spring in your step and all that crap. Honestly, I do.

Now read this book, would you? So I don't have to slap you.

CONTENTS

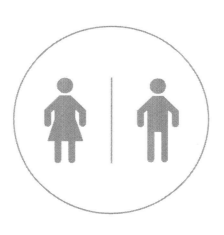

STARTING OUT

1

◯ FALL IN LOVE WITH SOMEONE ELSE FIRST

Perhaps the most challenging, frustrating and painful journey we embark upon in our lives is the search for someone to love – who will love us back. I hear from stacks of people who are in the throes of agony over their relationships, whether it's 15 months or 15 years down the line. There are stories of lies, heartbreak, betrayal, and indifference. And sadly, many people tolerate it for years on end, all in the name of "love."

Well, if you're in an unhappy relationship where you are being treated with disdain, disrespect or derision, you most certainly SHOULD fall in love with someone else.

YOURSELF.

If you do not love yourself first and foremost above all else, you will never be truly happy in a relationship. I'm not talking about selfish, narcissistic love or love at the expense of others.

What I mean is self-respect, acceptance, and appreciation for the person you are – warts and all.

When you love someone, you want only the best for them, right? You look out for their safety. You make sure they're well taken care of. You certainly don't want them to be hurt. These things are all pretty obvious, right? So why don't people treat themselves the same way?

Because they don't love themselves. They're not looking out for their best interests.

If you love yourself, respect who you are as a person, realize you are entitled to respect and honesty from others, you won't put up with crap! You won't accept it as "your fate" or "the best you can do."

You'll do something to change it. Talk about it. Get help from a counselor. If you love yourself, you do NOT continue to accept pain and heartache.

It's hard to develop confidence and self-belief in the face of adversity, but it is impossible without a strong foundation of love and respect for yourself. Love for yourself is what gives you the power to speak up, ask questions, seek help and change your circumstances.

And another thing! Until you know yourself, accept and understand your strengths and weaknesses, you cannot really love another person.

You must be filled with love yourself in order to love another. After all, you must have something to give! Otherwise, in a relationship, you'll suck. Suck the love from someone else and use it simply to fill up your void. I'm sure you've met some "suckers" in your life – I know I have. But until you know what makes your heart "tick," how can you entrust its care and feeding to someone else?

Here's the way I look at it, and maybe it will help you too.

I'm the queen of my heart. As queen, I expect to be treated with respect. In my realm, I will only allow people who value and appreciate me. No one will raise his hand up to me. I will not allow anyone who lies or cheats to live in my queendom. Those who break the rules will be punished by banishment, or I will pick up my queendom and move it someplace out of their reach. Crap, baggage and garbage will be swiftly discarded, lest my queendom become stinky. I will only give my precious heart to someone who can demonstrate he can take care of it the way I do: with care, respect, understanding and appreciation. And I will ALWAYS lead by example.

After all, how can you expect others to love, respect and honor YOU if you don't yourself?

2

WHAT DO YOU MEAN YOU'LL "RUIN" THE FRIENDSHIP?

The other day someone said something that struck me as very funny. It's something I've heard over and over again, but for some reason, the significance finally hit me.

This lady said she knew a wonderful guy and really enjoyed being with him, they were growing closer, and were attracted to each other, but she wasn't sure she wanted to have sex with him because she didn't want to "ruin the friendship."

RUIN the friendship.

Do you realize what she's saying? What everyone who has ever said this is saying?

Growing closer and sharing love will RUIN a friendship. Finding a soul mate, with whom you can share your triumph, sadness, ups and downs will RUIN a friendship. Being intimate and committing yourself to another person will RUIN a friendship.

What does this say about how we view intimate relationships? Unions that should really be the greatest friendships of all?

Well, I guess we don't see our partners as friends – that's for sure.

Friends are fun to be with. Friends are open and honest with us. They don't lie; they tell us exactly how they feel. Friends understand we need time by ourselves sometimes, and if we don't call, it doesn't mean we're not still friends – we're just doing something else. Our friends accept us as we are, and don't compare us to old friends. We laugh about the time we had a disagreement. Or we just forget about it, but we certainly don't remind each other about it every time we get cranky.

With our good friends, we can talk about ANYthing. Or we can just hang out together and not say a word. We don't wish we could change our friends. We accept them as individuals, and like them just the way they are.

But as soon as a friendship becomes a relationship, oh my, all hell breaks loose.

We walk on eggshells. We can't say what we think because we don't want to hurt each other. We're afraid to be honest about our feelings. We agonize if they don't call every single day. We expect them to drop everything to be with us. To want to spend every moment with us.

To whom do we give the greater respect? Friends or lovers? I know what the answer seems to be, and what it SHOULD be.

When you "cross that line" into intimacy, your friendship should deepen and become stronger. Ideally, you are making a commitment to be intimate only with that one person.

You are saving that special part of your relationship for each other. And with it comes other emotional intimacy.

But fergawdsakes you should still be FRIENDS.

Perhaps what this lady meant was, what if we sleep together, and he looks dorky naked or we don't click physically – will we be able to "go back" to just friends? "Just" friends.

But of course! If you are truly friends, you respect each other. You can laugh about your silly mistakes. You can put them in the amusing memories file (the one that only gets accessed after one or two cocktails), and move on.

A good friendship is rare and valuable. It's worth the effort. And most important, it should form the basis of a good, healthy intimate relationship. Whatever else you are together, you must be FRIENDS. Respect each other's individuality. Appreciate each other's differences. Demand and deliver honesty, loyalty and integrity. Do all of this, and your friendship will remain unshakable. A little nookie might make it better, it might not make any difference at all, but it certainly won't make a dent.

3

DATING SITES ARE A-WASTE-OF-TIME.COM

When I was young(er) and searching for love, people went out to bars, pubs, dances, gyms, grocery stores and bowling alleys to meet other people. You met someone, you chatted, you sized them up a bit, and decided whether you would be interested in being with that person again – because really the primary reason people want to get into a relationship is to be with someone. There was no guarantee that person would be the right person, but at least if they were shoveling a load of BS in your direction, they did it to your face.

It's different now. Nowadays millions of people prefer to shop for potential mates like they shop for airline tickets – searching through pages and pages of online listings containing thumbnail photos and earnest (though mostly lame) attempts at amusing, intriguing or sincere descriptions. They must broadcast their most personal qualities and intimate desires in a prepackaged resume in the hopes of initiating a tentative email exchange with a like-minded lonely heart until god-knows how long before they finally bite the bullet and meet up.

I just don't get it. I absolutely do not see how this is preferable to meeting someone in the flesh. First of all, most people don't write as well as they think or speak (except for me, of course). Secondly, an email exchange is not a give and take conversation. It's a chess game. It doesn't happen in real time, and it's not the way you're going to relate to that person in a real relationship. Thirdly, being online does not make you any more desirable. Jerks, creeps, psychos, gold-diggers, control freaks and slugs are not magically transformed. They are exactly the same. Except they can lie about themselves much more easily.

I hear the ads. I see the supposed "proof." I guess some matches have been made online. But that doesn't mean it's a great solution. Matches are made in every odd situation you can think of. People meet during catastrophes. But you don't see companies springing up, offering to drop you into the path of a train wreck with the promise of finding your true love.

Every person I know who has tried an online dating service has had exactly the same sort of experience they would have had if they'd met offline. You meet one or two nice folks, a bunch of losers, perhaps someone to date for a while, and maybe, just maybe you meet your match.

But at least the old-fashioned way, you got to go out and DO something! You got to dress up and try a restaurant or see a movie or visit an art gallery. You got out in the fresh air or under the stars and experienced life in all its three-dimensional fullness. You rolled the dice, you made an effort, and the other person did too – or maybe they didn't, which is why you never see them again, but AT LEAST you got out and tried.

Online, no one has to try very hard. And maybe that's the appeal. You don't invest much, so you don't feel bad if you don't get much in return. You send a couple emails, big deal. You don't have to interrupt your schedule. You don't have to find a sitter, or get your hair done.

It's all just a bit of harmless diversion. Or a game. Hmm. Sounds to me just like the classic singles bar. We've simply transferred a set of behaviors from a real-life location to a virtual one. One with even less honesty, effort or initiative. I can't see how it's an improvement.

My friends, I am often asked where one should look to find the right person. The only answer I can give is, don't look. Be. Learn how to be yourself. Find out how to be happy. Go out and do the things you enjoy doing. Learn something new. Try a new activity. You will find people who enjoy doing the same things. And they'll see you. After all, there is nothing more attractive than seeing someone do something they're passionate about. But you can't see that online.

4.

BEING A "FRIEND WITH BENEFITS" HAS FEW

There is a curious sub-set of friendship that seems to have become popular of late. It's called "friends with benefits." It means, "you're just my buddy, and I'm not really interested in you romantically (or frankly, even attracted to you), but on those occasions when we get really sloshed, or we both end up alone (but together) on a Saturday night, we can bonk our brains out and not be weirded out in the morning."

I'm sorry, but I just think it's a cheap cop-out. And what's more, it demeans the friendship, not to mention potential romance. It's like having an escort service you don't have to tip.

And here's a point of view that's going to piss some folks off: I think shagging with any old friend or acquaintance just for the heck of it kind of goes against nature. Here's why.

From an "anthropological" standpoint, our species evolved around long gestation of offspring, and helplessness at birth. According to Bill Bryson, in "A Short History of Nearly Everything," when our prehistoric precursors developed a pelvis sturdy enough to allow them to walk upright, it also resulted in a comparatively small birth canal, which meant in order to fit through it, babies would have to be born with small brains and little ability to be self-sufficient. As a result, infants required long-term care, which implies solid male-female bonding. After all, someone has to be getting the food if someone else is staying back at the cave with the kid.

So what does this mean? It means whatever your religious or cultural beliefs, our species was designed to pair up, make babies and stick together to raise them. Messing around for sport serves no particular anthropological need. Although it is fun.

But it's not what we're wired for, really. Deep in our bones, when we have sex, it means something. In our most ancient, primeval memory, it's part of bonding and procreation. It's what we are meant to do.

So as a result, I think there are two things wrong with "friends with benefits:"

1.   It's really, really hard to stop yourself from having feelings of belonging or "possession" about people you've slept with (more than once). Even the coldest Don Juan is going to feel some sort of privileges or power over a woman he's been with multiple times. And I think for women, it's even more so. We find it even more difficult to detach our hearts from our southern hemispheres.

A one-night stand is one thing. When the planets are properly (or improperly) aligned, stuff happens. Things seem like a great idea. A couple of cocktails with a shot of moonlight and a slow-dance chaser, and the next thing you know, your underpants are inside out.

But if you keep dipping into the same well again and again, you're bound to feel some ownership or sense of belonging. It can't help but change the friendship. It will either develop into something more (whether you want it or not), or one of you will feel hurt or strange when the other embarks on a "real" romantic relationship. The chances of two people being able to balance a perfect equilibrium of neutrality are slim indeed. If you both insist it's truly a friendship – with extras – I have a sneaking suspicion someone (or two?) is either feeling a lot more, or a lot less, than he or she is willing to admit.

2.   Relegating intimate sexual contact to just "benefits" cheapens and degrades a most wondrous form of expression. If it's "just sex" with one person, how do you flip the switch and turn it into something more with another? And why turn your great friend into a convenience? Don't you value the friendship more than that? Or the person? You say you care about each other as friends, but obviously not enough to make a real commitment – or worse yet, be seen together in public as a couple. But when you're stuck together watching some lousy rerun on Showtime, you'll go at it like rabbits. What a deal. You don't have to pay for a date, worry about calling the next day or even dressing up.

I know it's not a perfect world, but in a perfect world, sexual intimacy is an expression of love and caring between two people, and just one part of a deep, respectful relationship. I also know that very often it isn't the case. But the closer you get to that goal (on a consistent basis), the happier you will be. On the banquet table of life, trying to make sex just one a la carte selection with a friend or passing acquaintance may seem appetizing, but it won't quell your hunger long term.

In my opinion, casual sex with friends is the doughnut of romance. You may think it's tasty now, but you'll pay for it later.

I have a theory that human nature has been basically unchanged for the last few thousand years. The way we deal with each other, our drives and desires have all been fairly consistent. In prehistoric times, I imagine our communication was fairly simplistic: Are you friend or foe? Can I eat you, or mate with you?

Through the eons, we moved from simple animal communication, to conversation and discourse, with great subtlety of meaning, and beauty of expression. But there's one thing that drives me nuts. At what point in our evolution, did we lose the ability to simply ask for what we want? When did our communication skills devolve into mumbling and vagueness?

Let me illustrate the point with a sandwich.

So imagine this attractive lady sitting down in a restaurant. She wants a sandwich. The hunky waiter comes over and thinks, "Gee, that's a very attractive lady there. Glad I got her table." The lady looks at the waiter and thinks, "Boy, is he hunky. I bet he knows what I want." So she says, "I'd like to order a sandwich." The waiter thinks to himself, "I can't wait to serve her" and says, "It'll be right up."

The waiter goes back to the kitchen thinking, "I'm going to impress her by golly. I'm going to make her my most favorite sandwich in all the world: liverwurst and ham with extra mustard and onions. Boy, will she be impressed."

Meanwhile, the lady is eagerly anticipating the sandwich, "I bet he'll bring me my favorite turkey with tomato and jack cheese. He looks so perfect. I'm sure he knows exactly what I want."

After a moment, the waiter appears with the sandwich. He smiles shyly. She smiles back. And with a little flourish, he grandly sets the sandwich in front of his fair maiden.

SHE: "Eeeeeeuuuw! What the heck is THAT!"

HE: "Why it's a sandwich. My absolute favorite in all the world."

SHE: "But that's not what I wanted! I wanted turkey and tomato and jack cheese."

HE: "But you just said 'sandwich.'"
SHE: "But you're supposed to know."

Can you imagine if restaurants were like relationships? Luckily, they're not. In restaurants we order precisely what we want, and most of the time we get exactly that. In relationships, we expect our partners to figure things out by osmosis, the cellular transfer of thought particles.

If the lady in the restaurant had ordered a turkey sandwich with tomato and jack cheese, and the waiter had presented it to her, I bet you they'd be canoodling somewhere right now. When we care for someone, we love giving them exactly what they're looking for, right?

But we only know what they want if we ask, and of course if we ask, they must tell us. This is not a problem limited to men or women. We ALL fall into this trap.

"But you're supposed to know." Be honest, you've said it, and you've heard it. But be fair. How are you ever going to know if no one tells you? Don't be afraid to say what you want. The scary thing is, you may actually get it.

6

○ MAKE SURE
YOU SHARE
THE SAME
PASSIONS

I was out having some "margs" with a friend of mine (as you do), and we were discussing men (as you do). In particular, we were talking about characteristics of various partners, past and present and how they looked "on paper."

It's a funny thing about ratings "on paper." They tend to include the assorted qualities and attributes we think we should have, those we've been told we should have by numerous sources: our parents, our friends, the media. It's all the usual stuff: good family, good job, education, reliable, hard-working. I'm not denying those qualities are admirable and desirable.

But I think there are some other things that are sadly overlooked. Where does it say, "likes to give backrubs" or "laughs at stupid things" or "loves chocolate ice cream as much as I do"? On which important checklist do you ever see, "shares my passion for sunsets" or "loves model railways"? In our hearts we look for those things, but sometimes when we actually meet someone and evaluate them as potential mates, we forget—to our detriment.

Granted, we live in a time of luxury for the most part – luxury of choosing our careers, where we live, who we love. Luxuries previous generations never had (and some cultures don't have to this day). (And at the risk of digressing, I'll add that previous generations didn't have the luxury of "selfishness" - leaving everything behind, starting anew and changing direction).

HOWEVER! Since we DO, I'd like to propose that our lists "on paper" are incomplete. After years of trial and error (mostly error), I realized I was overlooking some very key things. I was checking the list for the rational qualities, but completely ignoring my passions. Those interests that made my heart race, pleasures I ranked above all others, activities I'd choose to do any day of the year.

And my point of view is, if you cannot do those things with your official partner, you'll either find someone else to share them with, one way or the other, or you'll be miserable.

There are a couple things I'm passionate about: diving and salsa. Maybe it's a weird mixture, but heck, it's me. I love to be on the water, and I love to dance. Well, finally I've hit pay dirt. I've met a man who enjoys those things as much as I do. My soul is fulfilled. On paper, we look like a funny match, but in spirit, we're in synch.

There's no one else I'd rather do my favorite things with. I don't have to sneak away, or steal time. I never feel guilty about indulging my favorite pleasures, because we do them together.

And that's the point. Yes, to an extent it matters if your partners look good on paper. But how do they look in your heart?

7

○ GET REAL

Over the holidays one year, a pal of mine was invited to a party, hosted by a man some friends wanted her to meet. It was a "blind date" of sorts, and of course she wanted to make an excellent first impression. In addition to going for a "full poodle" (make-up, nice hair, painted toenails), this also required bringing tasty and impressive dishes to the potluck.

Two things you need to know about my friend: 1. She's a tall, gorgeous blonde, but most days she'd rather dress in beat-up shorts, t-shirt and flip-flops, and 2. She really can't cook.

Knowing my predilection for the kitchen, she called me for help on point 2, and I was happy to oblige. I helped with the shopping list and guided her through the preparation process. She was on her own with the poodling, but had plenty of experience with that.

Off she went to the party, looking glam, bringing hand-made, home-cooked food.

And I got to thinking.

What happens if she likes this guy, and he likes her, and she has to invite him over? Will I need to be in the kitchen like a cooking "Cyrano de Bergerac" to her "Christian" for future meals? (What a pretentious reference, eh? Honestly, I'm not really that well-read. For the most part, I'm a cultural slob. Anyway...) What happens when he falls for the Glamazon in heels and meets up with the woman underneath?

In commerce, it's illegal to execute a "bait and switch." But in romance, we do it all the time.

I'm not suggesting we shouldn't make an effort in relationships, whether early on or after many years. I just think we should be true to ourselves. And be comfortable.

It's tricky. We like making an effort for special occasions. We want to make sure we look our best when it's important. But we also run the risk of setting expectations unrealistically high.

When you go to a job interview all dressed up, you present a view of yourself that your employer will expect you to maintain on a daily basis. And for the most part, it's possible, because your work day represents only a segment of your life (sometimes a HUGE segment, but that's another story).

On the other hand, a relationship should represent the primary segment of your life - encompassing morning face and bedhead at dawn, and post-dinner couch slumber at night. At some point, your partner is going to need to know you, and accept you "warts and all."

And yet, how many relationships would have EVER gotten off the ground without that artificially enhanced first impression? I think very few.

We're all susceptible to marketing. We want to buy into the promise, the carefully posed "beauty shot" - even if it is just a "serving suggestion." But as I've said before, in relationships, we mustn't fall in love with the dream, but the reality. We need to introduce our potential partners to our true selves sooner rather than later.

As for my friend, the party was fine, but sparks didn't fly between her and the host, which I suppose in retrospect, isn't surprising. After all, who exactly did he meet?

8

You know all those pictures and models of dinosaurs you see in museums? Do you ever wonder how paleontologists figured out what the animals looked like when all they had was a couple of bones to go by? It's simple. They guessed. They just filled in the blanks.

I sometimes think romance and paleontology are related. When we meet someone new, we know only a few bits of information about them. We might know where they work, how they dress, what kind of car they drive. On the first date or so, we get some insight into their personality. We might even have a first kiss.

But all we really have is a few bones. Now be honest.

I know you've done this. You come home after the first date – or maybe even the fourth date – and you start reconstructing your dinosaur.

You make a bunch of assumptions. You fill in some blanks. You sprinkle in some wildest dreams, and voila! You've got a complete model. You've built the perfect person! Based on a few data points and a bunch of wishful thinking, you project your desires on the little bit you know, and fill in all the blanks with everything you want.

The problem is, slowly but surely, you begin to fall in love with your creation, and what's more, believe it is the truth. Naturally, the object of all this fantasy has absolutely no idea he's been "reconstructed." He just keeps plodding on, being the person he is. Sooner or later though, he'll do something that doesn't match your blueprint. But it's not his fault you're disappointed – it's yours. After all, you created the monster. When you meet someone new, you must be very, very careful you do not project a perfect image on a perfect stranger.

Of course, we don't only have this problem with people we've just met. We often fill in the blanks with people we know very well. I don't think love is necessarily blind. I just think it doesn't always recognize the difference between reality and fantasy.

Here's reality (check all those that apply): He doesn't call very often. He won't tell you he loves you. He spends a lot of time away – in another city or country.

He hasn't left his wife yet. He's the father of your child, but he's not around much. You generally only get together after meeting at a bar. He says he's confused about his feelings.

Here's fantasy: I know he really means well. He must care about me – we have such a connection in bed. He wouldn't keep coming back if he didn't care. I know we'd be perfect together. He just needs more time.

Fantasy is all about what could be, what might be. It's not about what IS. You must be careful that you're not trying so hard to see into the future, you miss what's happening in the present.

Because in a relationship, all you can do is deal with the present. What am I getting out of this now? How is he behaving towards me today? The past doesn't matter, and the future is unknown. What's important is this moment, without embellishments, without filling in the blanks or assumptions.

In paleontology, we dig up bones and reconstruct an image to try to imagine what was. But in love we try to imagine what will be. Hopes and dreams are wonderful things. They inspire us to work hard and achieve. But you cannot fall in love with what you HOPE a person might be. You must love what they are today. No bones about it.

9

SET YOUR EXPECTATIONS CORRECTLY

So many disappointments in life could be avoided if our expectations were set correctly in the first place. I suppose it's our desire to please that makes us set expectations unrealistically, expectations that are doomed to disappoint. They happen in two ways: either someone says something that sets an (ultimately incorrect) expectation, or you develop an expectation that the other person cannot deliver.

Setting the expectation
I can't tell you how many times I've been cheesed off because my expectation was set incorrectly. "It will be done on Tuesday." "I'll have it finished in two weeks." "We'll be there at 2:00." Or the worst one of all: "I'll call you next week." Aaaaack. You know exactly what I mean, right? Someone tells you something, or

makes an arrangement, and you dutifully note it, and prepare for it, and then it never happens, or happens late with no explanation, let alone an apology. It drives me friggin' nuts.

Don't promise me one thing because it's what you think I want to hear. Promise me what you know you can deliver. It's not just in relationships,; it's in every aspect of life! You're going to eventually get fired if you never deliver on your commitments. We wouldn't keep hiring someone to do work if they never delivered when they said they would, would we?

In order to achieve results, achievable goals must be set. If it's going to take two weeks to finish a project, promise it in two weeks – or even three weeks, but don't promise one week just to make someone happy. You'll make that person very UNhappy when you miss the deadline. You'll destroy their trust, damage your goodwill and lose a customer – or a friend.

On the other hand, if you promise three weeks, and do it in two, you'll fill that same person with unbridled, sweaty joy.

Just be honest. Why is that so hard? Why can't you just say the truth? And if you're going to have to change a deadline, or miss an appointment, or cancel a date, call and let me know! Aren't these things simply common courtesy? When did people stop learning these skills? When did business people stop acting professionally? When did everyone stop knowing how to treat friends and associates? Sigh. Of course it's not all your fault. I'll admit it. It could be my fault too.

Developing an expectation
We all like to indulge in a little daydreaming now and then. And fantasizing. It's fun to think of what could be, and what we wish for. The problem is, we often take these wishes and turn them into expectations of reality.

It goes something like this:
- He's cute.
- He's so cute, he could be the man of my dreams.
- We've gone out, and by golly, he really seems to be the man of my dreams.
- The man of my dreams would call me back the next day.
- If he's the man of my dreams, then WHY HASN'T HE CALLED ALREADY?

Who said he was the man of your dreams? Why, you did. You made it all up. You assumed something, right? And you know what happens when you assume? You make an "ass" out of "u" and "me."

When you assume something, you're setting unfair expectations. You're setting an expectation the other party knows nothing about. The other party doesn't even know he was carrying the ball you think he dropped. You can't get mad. It was actually your fault.

I am generally a positive person, but I am also generally pretty cynical. For the most part, I try to keep my expectations low for other people (not for myself, but for others). I don't expect the moon. I expect a little asteroid here and there. Or a shapely rock, but not the whole moon. It prevents me from being disappointed. Sometimes I do get the whole moon. And I can tell you, when all I expected was a rock, getting the whole moon is a wonderful, wonderful thing.

We cannot force others to set correct expectations. People are always going to promise one thing and deliver another. But we can change our own expectations. If you always expect the absolute best, you will often be disappointed. Set realistic expectations, and dreams may come true.

When most of us are facing difficult or complicated decisions, we like to seek the counsel of others. Heck, you probably wouldn't be reading my little ramblings if you weren't also in that subset of humanity. As am I.

I like to get various, if not opposing, viewpoints on stuff. It helps me make an informed decision – even though I know at the end of the day, it's going to come down to me to make the decision.

When I'm making tough decisions, I particularly like to ask "neutral observers" – people outside my circle who won't be affected one way or t'other by my decision. If possible, I like to seek someone who has experience in the particular arena I'm dealing with.

Sounds obvious, doesn't it? Well let me tell you a little story.

A couple hundred years ago, a man happened to walk past young Ben Franklin's house (yes, THAT Ben Franklin). The man stopped to admired Ben's dad's grindstone and asked him to show him how it worked. Young Ben obliged. Then the man pulled out his own axe to see a real-life demonstration. Ben gladly sharpened the axe, and gave it back to the man, who walked away laughing. You see, the man needed to sharpen his tool, and had no one to turn the stone. In other words, he had an ulterior motive to begin with: he had an axe to grind.

When you ask someone close to you for advice, be very, very aware they may also have an axe to grind. For example, do your friends always tell you moving far away is a very bad decision? Not surprising. They don't want to be alone.

Does your husband tell you going back to school or re-entering the workforce is the wrong thing to do? Perhaps he doesn't want the competition.

Does your best friend tell you you're new boyfriend is bad news? Maybe she's afraid of losing your friendship.

When you ask for advice and counsel, always consider the source. From whom do you want to take fashion advice? A catwalk model, or a slob? Who do you think will give the best financial advice? The gas station attendant, or Donald Trump? And who has a more vested interest in your decisions: your family, your close friends, your mentors or your co-workers?

But of course that's only part of the issue. It's possible to get wonderful and lousy advice from the same person, at different times, regardless of their relation to you. Your family and friends may know you best of all, and sometimes understand you better than you do yourself. A neutral observer may have experience that has no relevance to your situation. I may be an expert on relationship issues, but I can assure you I'm clueless when it comes to recommending power tools. But we're not really talking about impact wrenches, nibblers and reciprocating saws. We're talking about you.

It doesn't matter who is giving you advice if they're not really giving you advice about the true heart of the matter. When the time comes for you to make decisions about key events in your life, you must first boil down the decision to the fundamental desire you wish to get from the decision.

The most valuable advice you can get from anyone is feedback or direction about how your decision will affect your ability to get specifically what you want. Everything else is extraneous. But first you need to identify what your fundamental desire is.

For example, you're not happy in your marriage because sex is no good with your husband. You can't tell him how you feel. So you're considering having an affair. You think the question is really "should I have an affair or not?" Actually, that's not the question at all. The question really is, "Do I want to be married to this man or not?"

You can sit with your friends for hours and debate the issue of infidelity when that's not really the decision you need to make. Do you want to be with your husband, or not? Do you want to do everything in your power to work together to fix the issue, or not? If not, then don't be married to him! You'll be free to pursue all manner of flings and forays to your heart's content. (Of course, I'll bet when you go through this exercise, you'll discover you don't really want more sex, but more emotional intimacy, and that's a different story).

When we are faced with a decision, there is generally one primary thing we are hoping for, which we hope the decision will bring about. Your job as decision-maker is to clearly identify that one thing, and then evaluate which of your options will best deliver your wish. No matter what anyone else says or wants, you must make the decision that suits YOUR need. And before you can make any decision, good or bad, you must ensure you understand what that need is.

11

I'd like to talk to you about trust in relationships. But first I have to get something else off my chest.

I cannot tell you how many emails I've gotten from people who start out by saying something like, "I love my husband/boyfriend and can't imagine leaving him, BUT" (choose one from the following list):

- He hardly gives me any attention.
- Nothing I do is good enough.
- He spends a lot of time on the computer chatting with other women.
- He promises he's broken off the affair.
- He lives in another state and we only see each other once a month.

Does any of this sound familiar to you? Do any of you see any inconsistencies between the first sentence and the rejoinders?

You DON'T?

Well, what exactly DO you love about this person? What are you getting out of the relationship? If your answers have anything to do with security, finances or a roof over your head, you're not in love; you're in business.

It's not so much the definition of love I have a problem with; it's the definition of a healthy loving relationship. Sure it's possible to love things about someone, but it doesn't necessarily mean it's possible to have a healthy, loving relationship with them. All of the rejoinders in the list above? Not signs of a healthy, loving relationship. No matter how much you love that person, he (or she) is not demonstrating love for you back. No matter how much you want it to be so, it is NOT healthy, loving behavior. Either you work with your partner to fix or change it, or you end the relationship.

Okay. Now where was I? Oh yes. Trust.

Relationships must be built on a very solid foundation of trust. Rock solid. You cannot spend all your time peering around corners, or checking phone records, or going through pockets. You must trust.

But it's a funny thing – although trust must be rock solid, it is by nature ethereal. It's like faith. You must believe.

You cannot know what someone is doing every minute of the day when he or she is not with you. You cannot sit inside someone's head and listen to every thought. Lies often sound the same as the truth.

But if you're in an open, honest relationship, there should be no cause for worry. And here's the important part. In an open, honest relationship there is no inconsistency between what he says, and what he does. No behavior makes you feel a bit funny. Nothing raises a red flag. There are no things that make you go, "hmm."

I trust my sweetie because there is nothing in his behavior to make me think otherwise. He is consistent in word and deed. And equally important, I am getting everything out of the relationship I want.

If you are satisfied in your relationship, if your sweetie's behavior is completely consistent (i.e. calls when promised, never has funny excuses or stories, or disappears for days at a time), what are you worried about? Either this person is fantastically adept at juggling multiple relationships at once or is actually telling the truth.

As an expert on farm animals once said, "If it walks like a duck, swims like a duck, and quacks like a duck, it probably is a duck." And that goes both ways.

If something doesn't feel right in your gut, if a story doesn't sit well, or promises are consistently broken, blind trust is probably not a good idea. You're right to feel funny, and you're entitled to ask questions. If you don't get the truth back, or something that feels like the truth, don't let the behavior continue. And if you can't change his behavior, change yours. Leave.

It may not be the solution you were looking for. You were probably hoping for honesty, and truth, and sunshine and birds tweeting happily ever after. But unfortunately, it doesn't always work out that way.

If your relationship doesn't make you feel good most of the time, it's not a good relationship. Which brings me back to the very beginning of this ramble.

It's one thing to trust and believe the reality you're experiencing is indeed reality. It's quite another to trust and believe the dream you have for your relationship might change the reality. I know I say this all the time, but I have to say it again. Make sure you're in love with the REALITY, not the dream. Trust me on this.

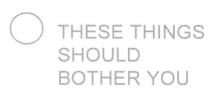

12

It's a good thing fires produce smoke, so we have some sort of early warning system of impending danger, don't you think? Smoke tells you there's fire, which means you need to get out of the way, and sooner rather than later, I might add. Because fire isn't just hot – why, it can burn you, can't it? And even scar you for life. And destroy everything you hold dear. I don't think I need to hammer this home any further, do I? It's blooming obvious, isn't it?

But not when it comes to relationships, apparently.

Warning signs in relationships are no less obvious, yet we seem completely oblivious! Every single one of the samples I'm including below, I've received in emails - many times over. How can it not be obvious that something is not altogether ideal in these relationships? Perhaps it's because we don't actually see them as red flags. Well, if that is indeed the case, I shall provide you with a handy guide as to WHY these things are cause for alarm, and why they should bother you – a lot.

You only see each other during the week – never on weekends. Generally, weekends are a time for pleasure and leisure (unless we have to work on weekends). We take part in our favorite activities on weekends, with our favorite people. Why are you not in that category? If you're in a real relationship, you should be. You should be his priority. Is there someone else in that top spot? Are you comfortable on the "B" list?

He has never invited you to his place. What secret is he keeping? Is it just that he's a terrible slob, or is it because someone else lives there with him – someone he wants to hide from you? Or is he just selfish? In a give and take relationship, you should be sharing – and that includes sharing some of his life.

Although he professes love over the phone, and you've visited him, he has never visited you. If he really, really cares, wild horses shouldn't be able to keep him away – unless he's stationed overseas, of course. But even if your relationship has to be long distance, there must be some initiative on his part to see you – and call you. If it's all one-sided now, I can promise you it will NEVER get any better.

You've never met any of his friends. If this is a person with whom you want to share your life, you'll want to share HIS life too. If you're a real couple, you're integrated into each other's lives and do things together. Sure, you do things without each other too, and you may prefer to let him hang out with his buds on his own, but you should be able to meet them if you want to.

When you're together you have great sex, but otherwise you never go out. It's true, sex is cheaper than most other entertainment, and if you have limited time together, it may seem more appealing than sharing a pizza, but a relationship with someone must be based around more than just sex. You'll be living in the real world with this person – you need to experience the real world with him too. And the real world exists outside the bedroom. If you can't afford dinner and a movie, take a walk. Get to know each other vertically as well as horizontally.

He's in prison. I know people make mistakes, and do move on from them. But when you're meeting someone new, it's like interviewing him for a job. You look at his resume and experience to be a predictor of future success. Of all the people in the world you can choose for the job of holding your heart, is this the right person? Does he have a history of honesty, clean living and reliability? If not, do you really want to take the risk? Why not give him a chance to get out, and start his life over, before you commit to him.

In the time he's been seeing you, he has fathered a child with someone else. And chances are, you have a child with him too! Is it too obvious to say this is not a good way to start a family? This man has no sense of responsibility – and he's a liar and a cheat besides. And by the way, having more children with him will not fix the problem, in case you were hoping.

Since he's been living with you, he's been unemployed. In general, we humans respond well to satisfying needs. After all, the cavemen went out and hunted because they were hungry. They discovered fire because they were cold. If you satisfy all your caveman's needs, he's not going to be doing much hunting and gathering. He has no need. But what would he do if you weren't there? Mooch off of someone else, or make an effort? And if the only answer is he'd mooch off someone else, why do you want to be with someone like that?

He still lives with his mother. If he's over 21, heck to be honest, if he's over 18 (and not in college full time), it's about time this little bird spread his wings and flew the coop. You want a man who knows how to take care of himself, because then he'll know how to take care of you. You want a man who respects and honors his mother, not one who depends on her.

My friends, I hope this little guide will help you smell the smoke before you get burned. If these things don't bother you now, they should. And if there's something else bothering you about your current relationship, there's probably a good reason why it does.

13

WHAT'S THE RUSH?

A 22-year-old young man and his 20-year-old girlfriend are certain they want to be together forever and are planning their wedding date. A woman who has just filed for divorce wants to know when it's ok to start dating again. Two divorcees I know met less than a year ago, live in different states, and are already engaged.

What's the rush?

I never understand this overwhelming, hurried urge to merge. Yes, it's nice to be in a relationship and have someone to love, but why hurry into marriage? Considering it's fairly common knowledge that more than half of all marriages fail, I guess more than half the population ignores the statistics! (But then again, people still actually smoke cigarettes.)

Whenever anyone asks me if I'm going to get married (again), my answer is always, why? I just can't find a reason that still holds true:

Social approbation – It used to be that single women or divorcees were shunned by society, but not any more. Likewise, "living in sin" was a big deal. Not in my social circles.

Economics – I always try to live within my means and assume I'm going to have to take care of myself. Personally, I could never imagine marrying for money or looking for someone to "take care of me." I suppose there are tax advantages and things like spouse's medical benefits – maybe it would be better to form a corporation!

Sex – Does anybody really marry so they can have sex? I thought that's what people did to STOP having it!

Companionship – You certainly don't need a marriage license for that.

Children – Now, THIS is a good reason. If I were going to have children, I'd want to be married. But my clock is just about ticked out, so it's not much of an issue for me. (However, just for the record, I'm very sad that so many couples, particularly young ones, end up creating new lives while having no clue how to run their own.)

The other puzzle to me is why folks want to rush into something to which they are hopefully committing the rest of their lives. Wouldn't you want to think about it a bit? See how it goes? I mean, it's not like there's an expiration date. Or the sale only lasts 'til the end of the month.

I've known women who pressure their men to "(spit) or get off the pot." Because they DO want children, and they figure they better get going sooner rather than later. I understand that. And I suppose the fellow's reluctance to commit is a pretty big red flag.

But otherwise, why not keep things going just as they are? Ride the waves a bit together. Let the relationship (and yourselves) mature. For young people starting out, I think it's critical to allow yourself to "be" on your own and define your individuality FIRST. For those of us further down the road, and especially just coming out of a relationship, we need to reclaim our individuality and ensure we've learned the lessons of the past so we don't make them all over again. And that takes time. How much? I dunno. But it's not as soon as possible.

14

○ AND YOU CALL THIS A RELATIONSHIP?

It appears to me many people seem to have some confusion over what a relationship is, how to form one, determine if they are actually in one, and finally how to keep it going.

Let's start with the basics. Most stable contented relationships are between two people. TWO. Not three. Not two, and another one online. Not two, and another one I only see once a month or so for sex only. Just two. It's fairest to both parties and accepted by most cultures over the centuries as a divine union.

Whether you have one of each gender, or a matched pair, the point is, for the most part, a party of two seems to be the optimal configuration. Relationships tend to work best when there's just the two of you to sort things out.

So I was surprised when a woman was surprised that her marriage suffered when she and her husband brought a third party into their relationship. HELLO! Even when they supposedly both agreed to knowingly screw up their relationship, they were shocked when it did in fact screw it up. Duh.

I simply don't get these people who say they happily subscribe to "polyamory." I don't buy it. I don't believe you can be fully present emotionally to more than one person at a time. It's mathematically impossible. There is only one YOU to go around. You cannot give 100% to three people at once.

Relationships are SUPPOSED to be about total commitment, honesty, and intimacy. We long to be linked to one person because it feels great to have a bond, a devoted partner and a caring lover. It's not just about sex, but good sex is an important component. And that's the tricky part.

Bad sex generally means it's a bad relationship. But good sex can happen without any relationship at all.

Another woman told me she wasn't sure whether she should continue seeing this man who came to her only when he wanted sex. Well, why not? Perhaps she should start charging him and make their time together a bit more worthwhile, because she certainly wasn't getting a "relationship."

If all you're getting is sex, no matter how fabulous, you're not in a relationship. You're having a booty call. If you have great sex, but your partner cannot understand and respond to your emotional needs, you're not in a healthy relationship.

Is it really that easy to simply have sex without the trappings of a relationship? Without emotion? Generally, I think not. If sex were that inconsequential, that easy to dismiss, how come so many people can't talk about it? Why would we be so concerned when the sex in our relationships changes, or becomes much less frequent?

Because it's HUGELY important, that's why. Sex is the barometer and the mirror of your relationship. If there is an imbalance in your relationship, chances are there will be an imbalance in your sex life too. If all he wants to do is look at porn and never look at you, I'll bet you never converse during dinner either. If you're not able to understand each other's sexual needs and figure out a way to satisfy each other, you probably argue about finances too. If you just can't seem to muster up any interest in physical intimacy, you may well be either unhappy with your partner, or unhappy with yourself.

 If you are able to communicate openly and intimately with your partner, your sex will be good as well. Sex is the most intimate form of communication we have. If you can make conversation, you can make love. (I was going to say, if you can communicate, you can fornicate, but it doesn't quite have the same ring to it).

The point is: you can have sex without a relationship, but it's very difficult to have a good, healthy relationship without sex. Now I know I'm going to get tons of emails from people who are in happy, loving platonic relationships telling me I'm full of luncheon meat. But let me answer right now. I think you are the exception, not the rule. And then there will be those who tell me they are abstaining from sex for various reasons, which I respect.

But for the vast majority in garden-variety monogamous relationships, or for those who aspire to be in one, the rule applies. ·

So if you're lucky enough to be in a relationship with another person (ONE other person), how do you stay that way? It's so simple really. TALK to them for goodness sake. Let them know how you're feeling. Ask them how they're feeling. And be honest when they ask you.

Your partner should be the absolute best authority on giving you advice as to how to satisfy his or her needs. After all, why would you ask a stranger where to scratch? Only your partner really knows where it itches.

KEEPING IT GOING

1

I'LL SAY IT AGAIN: RELATIONSHIPS TAKE EFFORT

Someone once gave me a wonderful analogy about relationships, which I'd like to take the liberty of sharing here. It goes something like this. Let's say you work for some imaginary company. You've got a pretty good job, and you don't mind getting up every morning to do it. One day, the CEO calls everyone together for a meeting and announces from that point on official company hours will be 9 am-10 am ONLY. That's it. From now on, you'll actively work on the business only one hour per day.

Pretty crazy, isn't it? How can you possibly expect to build a successful business, working just one hour a day? Well of course you can't. Nobody tries to build a business with so little effort. But here's the key point: lots of people try to build a relationship that way. Is it any wonder so many fail?

You know, it's funny. Just about everyone I've ever met in my entire life has wanted, or is still wanting, to be loved. After the fundamentals of food and shelter are taken care of, love is the thing we desire most. And yet so many don't want to work for it. Don't want to put any effort into retaining it. Or worse, don't even understand that it DOES take effort. And it certainly takes more than an hour a day.

But an hour a day is all many couples share with each other – if that. After you take out hours for sleep, work, commuting, taking care of the kids, homework, watering the plants, doing the laundry, what's left? I know it's hard to find time to do anything, let alone focus on your mate. But you must.

Relationships take some effort. They don't just take care of themselves. After all, a relationship is made up of you and another person. If neither of you is at the steering wheel, who is? You need to be together and talk together. Not just about "stuff," but about each other, so you know how you're doing as a couple. Can you imagine going to the doctor for a check-up and your entire exam consisting of a discussion of last Monday's football game? You need to tell the doctor exactly what you're feeling, and he (or she) needs to listen. Don't you remember how much fun it was to "play doctor" when you were a kid?

But seriously folks, you can't possibly expect to keep

your relationship vibrant, fulfilling and alive unless you spend some time on it. It shouldn't be hard work, but it does take effort. At the risk of dangerously exceeding my weekly quota of analogies, I'll add another. Your relationship is like a houseplant. It needs tending. Regular watering, a little food, sufficient light and careful pruning now and then. Like a plant, you can't just ignore your relationship and hope it will flourish. Unless it's a cactus. And if you think that sounds appealing, try hugging one.

2

You know what happens when you assume, right? You make an "ass" out of "u" and "me." (See? I didn't "assume" you'd heard that before.)

For example, never assume somebody is going to take care of something if you haven't confirmed it ahead of time. Never assume somebody knows what time the meeting is, or where it is if you haven't reiterated it. And most importantly, where your relationship is concerned, never assume your partner knows how you feel.

Has anyone ever said "I love you" too often? I doubt it. We always just "assume." He knows I really care about him – I wouldn't pick up anyone else's socks! She knows I love her – I told her on Valentine's Day—last year.

When we were growing up, charades was one of those games we sort of grudgingly played at parties. And yet as adults, we play it all the time! For some reason, going through all the mental and physical gymnastics of trying to communicate a subtle nuance of feeling or desire is preferable to just SAYING it, fergawdsakes.

But it feels so good to hear it! I'm not advocating a routine or a specific number of times per month. But just like you spontaneously and easily say "hey, this IS good tasting tuna," feel free to let your sweetie know how much you care.

As you might imagine, I'm fairly talkative. Words rarely fail me. My sweetie, on the other hand, is quiet and soft-spoken. He's a man of few words, but they so often end up being the right ones, which brings me to a particularly lovely event from a past weekend.

I was planning our meal for Saturday night, and although I generally try to make all our dinners a bit of an occasion (candles, dim lighting), this Saturday was even more of an occasion because it was part of a holiday weekend. Plus we were having lobster (freshly caught by my honey, I might add). So as I bustled around the kitchen, simmering, poaching and whisking, for no apparent reason, my sweetie left to "do something."

He returned a few minutes later with a dozen roses.

When I asked him why, he replied simply, "Because I love you, baby." Was that great or what? And it's not the first time.

I got the message loud and clear. I was covered in warm fuzzies for the rest of the weekend and beyond. And I made sure he understood how I felt about him!

So please folks, don't assume those nearest and dearest know how you feel about them. TELL them. They'll love hearing it. You'll feel better. And chances are you'll get it back multiplied. Love begets love. After all, it's kind of like manure. Spread it around thick, and you'll reap a bountiful harvest.

3

○ QUIT STARING
AT YOUR
BEHIND

I hope you don't mind me getting personal, but I need to talk to you about your behind. I want you to stop focusing on it. And mine for that matter!

Of course I'm talking about your past, what's behind you. You need to let the past go. You're never going to be able to move forward in your life or your relationships if you continually focus on what's behind you.

One of the greatest annoyances for both men and women in relationships is when their partners "constantly bring up the past." It's not a healthy thing to do. There are basically three ways we inappropriately focus on our behinds.

1. **Bringing up past events in the current relationship.** Chances are, at some point, we're all going to step in it one way or the other in our relationships. The amount we step in varies of course, and with care and communication, we should be able to resolve the situation. So when your partner has made a conscious effort to apologize or modify behavior, there's simply no need to keep bringing up the issue again and again. Particularly every time you get in an argument. You've got to let it go. Unless it's something that isn't changing and comes up over and over again. Then of course you need to resolve it. But do not keep bringing up those past peccadilloes and using them to make a point.

2. **Comparing the current relationship to one in the past.** We all want to feel we're the center of our partner's attention. That no one else matters, and sometimes, nothing else matters. But every time you bring up a previous relationship, you're bringing a third person into the mix. It doesn't matter if the comparison is positive or negative. Your partner doesn't want to hear it. If there's something that was better in the previous relationship, you need to speak with your partner now about what you want changed. That's the issue, not that it was "better before." And if you have negative memories or anger about a past relationship, work through it internally or with a friend, not your partner.

She'll wonder why you still "care."

3. **Dwelling over past decisions or events that got you where you are today.** This is perhaps the hardest to avoid. It's called "regret." The older we get, the more mistakes we accumulate, and therefore, the more regret. As we have less time ahead, we focus more on the time behind. But it's a huge time waster. It sucks the energy out of you and takes time away from the work you need to do to move forward. You're never ever going to change the past! Get over it! But you have lots of power to change the future and give yourself the "present" you've always wanted.

So have I made myself clear? My friends, the only behind you should be focusing on is the curvy variety – whether it's making your own a bit more perky or watching someone else's.

4

YOUR RELATIONSHIP NEEDS TLC

I wonder how many happy children receive an adorable, floppy puppy at Christmas. Probably lots. I'll bet the moms or dads spent a considerable amount of time explaining the care and feeding of a puppy. How it has to be loved and nourished. How it's a long-term commitment, which requires time, effort and patience. And then, later that day, after all the thoughtful explanation, I'll bet a lot of the moms and dads either had a giant screaming match with their spouse or called up the ex to say through clenched teeth that it's time to pick up the kid and the damn dog. Sigh.

It's amazing (and amazingly sad to me) that we take better care of our relationships with our pets than we do with each other. Heck, we take better care of our PLANTS.

We all know you have to tend a plant if it's going to thrive. You have to prune it back sometimes. You might have to give it something to lean on. Above all, you need to water it regularly. You can't just buy a ficus, stick it in the room, and expect it to stay green forever – unless it's fake.

You can't have a cute, cuddly puppy and never feed it or play with it. It'll wander off to find someone who will.

We spend so much energy trying to find someone to love, trying to rope someone into commitment, and after we do, seem to think the work is over. My friends the work has just begun!

I get a lot of emails from people in established relationships wanting to know how to keep them fresh. Well, all you have to do is what you did to get them going in the first place! It really is that simple.

Did you go out to dinner? Dress up more often than not? Make sure you were freshly scrubbed and shaved before bed? Did you buy flowers or cards or little presents and leave mushy notes on the fridge?

Did you sit and talk for hours about your feelings and dreams? Did you decide you could forgo watching your favorite tv program so you could stare into your lover's eyes and make out on the sofa? Did you hang on your lover's every word and listen intently when you discussed everything you'd done since you saw each other last?

These things do NOT become boring after years and years in a relationship. WE become boring.

We stop trying. We stop doing much of anything. We get into the ugly daily grind of life and march along because that's the way life is. WHO SAYS???? Who says romance only happens at the beginning? Who says it all disappears after the first blush of love fades?

MISERABLE PEOPLE, that's who! People who, for whatever reason, stopped doing all those things to keep the fires burning.

I get all these emails from ladies telling me about the wonderful excitement they're feeling from some new paramour (someone who is inevitably NOT their current husband or boyfriend). Well of course it's exciting. But it doesn't mean he's any better than your current partner – he's just the one making the effort right now. And perhaps your husband has found some other woman who's willing the make the effort you're not…

I've said it a million times: relationships shouldn't be hard work, but they do take EFFORT. Love doesn't stay lit all by itself. We have to stoke the fire. It is an organic, living, breathing thing – because it's made by organic, living, breathing things. US.

Stop being so lazy. Get out of the habit of slobbing around the house and back in the habit of romance. I could see it happening to me. I work from home most of the time, so I rarely have to dress up. I can spend the entire day in my sweats, with my hair all on one side of my head. It's comfy, but I gotta tell you, it ain't attractive. I was even running errands in full slob mode. What the heck. Who's going to see me?

Well, I saw me. And I saw all these women all dolled up, and I looked at them enviously, and then realized I used to look like that too – when I made the effort.

When I made the effort, romance bloomed, and I was sexy. When my sweetie made the effort, I was all over him like a cheap suit. That's the way it works. It's a cycle that never has to end – unless YOU end it. Unless you stop trying.

If you're going to make a resolution this year, resolve to go backwards. Back to the way you USED to be in your relationship. Even for just one day a week, go back in time to your early days and do the things you used to do. Dress up. Take a walk. Buy a card. Light candles. Shave.

Take care of your puppy. And above all, remember you have to MAKE love. It doesn't make itself.

5

WANT IS VERY
DIFFERENT
THAN NEED

My sweetie is a wanted man. Not by the authorities, or the FBI, or Interpol. But by me. He's definitely wanted. However I must honestly say he's definitely not needed. Nope. Absolutely not. I don't need him at all.

Does that mean I'm a heartless (w)itch? Certainly not. It simply means I understand the difference between "want" and "need." Do you? You should.

I think too many relationships are ruined or fail because the participants base them on "need" rather than "want."

Frankly, I don't think you should really ever "need" anybody.

You need to be responsible for yourself and your own happiness. As an adult, you need to be able to take care of yourself. You should not need anyone to define who you are or make decisions for you. You certainly do not need anyone to validate your existence or make you whole. You need to make a life for yourself, based on your own dreams and aspirations. You don't need someone else for that.

You do need food, shelter, clothing and shoes. (You probably actually need only about 2 pairs of shoes, by the way – just in case you were reading this while also daydreaming about those black sandals that have a slightly different heel than the other 3 pairs of black sandals you already have). You need to take care of your health. You need to generate income somehow to support yourself, and perhaps a family.

And you can want someone to be there with you. You can want companionship, a playmate, a sounding board. You can want a lover and a friend. You can want to spend your entire life with someone, grow old and wrinkly – or just be old and wrinkly.

But need is a scary thing. If you need to have him call you more than once a day, or need to hear she loves you all the time, or need to be in a relationship, you don't just have a need, you have a problem.

A need like that means you have a hole in yourself that you need to fix first. Something has caused your lack of confidence or insecurity –whether it is a result of your upbringing or previous relationships. But the only one who can fix it is you. The only one who can make you whole is you.

You cannot and should not expect someone else to make you happy. As I say over and over again, you are responsible for your own happiness. Until you are content and happy with yourself alone, no one will be able to satisfy you. If you don't know what will make you happy in life, how will you ever know when you've got it?

Having a relationship or getting married is not the answer to your happiness. In fact, if you ask around, at least half of the people will tell you it was the beginning of their heartache, not the end.

If you can get rid of the notion of "needing" someone for a relationship, you will be a lot happier. Learning how to make yourself happy and being able to take care of yourself is a wonderful, liberating thing. Knowing you are beholden to no person, that should everyone around you suddenly disappear you would still be able to survive gives you enormous strength. Fear disappears, and in its place is peace.

Sometimes, in my idle moments, I like to go through little "what if" scenarios in my mind. I'll randomly pick something in my life and go through a little plan just in case. Like, what if I lose my job or what if a hurricane blows the roof off my townhouse, or what if my car gets smashed up. Then I think through the various options and come up with a plan I can file for later use.

Hopefully, I'll never need it, but simply the fact that I've thought it through makes me feel better.

I'm the happiest and most content I've ever been in my current relationship because I really don't need him. I've already thought through how I'll deal with retirement, or supporting myself, or whatever it is. But I love being with him. He makes my life better and richer. He lightens my day-to-day load and adds fun and pleasure. I don't need anything he gives me, but I certainly don't want it to end.

6

When do you know a relationship is over? How can you tell when the embers have finally glowed their last and no combustible fuel remains to be reignited? For me, it was the moment I heard my soon-to-be-ex-husband utter two little words.

"I'll try."

Those two words were at once dismissive, condescending and disinterested. I knew at that instant our marriage would not continue. More hours of counseling, weekends away and scribbling in journals wouldn't make a dent. It was time to say our farewells, divide up the record collection, and move on.

In love, as in all facets of life, simply trying is not enough. We must succeed. "I'll try" means there's a big looming probability it won't happen. In fact, it's almost a prediction of failure.

I'll try means "you should give me some credit for my vain attempt, but you know and I know the odds of this actually happening are microscopically low." "I'll try" is a flimsy, not even waterproof band-aid slapped on a gaping wound already showing signs of infection.

A long time ago (in a galaxy far, far away), I took to heart the words spoken by one of the last surviving Jedi masters. While Luke Skywalker struggled with his lightsaber training and promised to try a little harder, Yoda replied, "Try not. Do, or do not. There is no try."

"I will" signifies the intent to succeed. "I will" means the goal is acknowledged, and effort will, not may, but WILL be made to achieve it.

On the other hand, "I'll try" means I really don't think I can. To achieve success, you must first believe it's possible.

To make a relationship work you must do much more than try. You must succeed. If you always try to make someone happy, but they never are, you are probably in the wrong relationship. Either nothing you can ever do will ever make them happy (in which case, what are you doing with them?) or you simply do not have the ability to do the things that would make them happy (in which case, what are they doing with you?).

I don't believe there's anything wrong with admitting you're in the wrong relationship. We don't always make the right choices, and we don't always have the best information on which to base them.

But there is no point in wasting more time on time already wasted. If you or your partner can't or won't make the commitment to succeed, stop "trying." If you do not see tangible results of your efforts, move on.

There is nothing more frustrating than going 'round and 'round in circles in life without seeing progress. Life is all about progression and change. It happens in nature, science and technology. And it happens in ourselves. If you don't believe me, take out a picture of yourself from five years ago and then look in the mirror.

Moving forward is the essence of life. Simply making an effort is not enough. You must get results. But don't confuse the two. They don't always go hand in hand.

Stop promising yourself you'll try. Make a vow to succeed, and then surround yourself with others who are committed to moving forward as well. Time will not stand still. Why should you?

7

ARE YOU
SETTING
YOURSELF UP
FOR FAILURE?

They say that many people are more afraid of
speaking in public than they are of death. That may
well be true, but I think even more people are afraid
of success, particularly in relationships.

Lots of folks seem to find a sort of comfort in not
succeeding. I tried my best. It wasn't my fault. I just
have bad luck. I seem to only attract the losers. The
good ones are all taken.

The inability to find success is predictable, and it
appears to be a result of factors beyond our control. I
can't help it that he's married. It's not my fault he
drinks. I'm not the one without a job. He's the one not
calling me back.

It's almost easier to just let heartache and disappointment wash over you. Oh well, it's my lot in life. I guess it's just not going to happen for me.

We are creatures of habit. We are most comfortable maintaining the status quo. If we are used to being less than satisfied in our relationships, and unlucky in love, we tend to stay that way. There is much less pressure in sustaining a low-key, if unhappy, existence.

Success takes effort. It may require (gasp!) change or a new attitude. And once it is achieved, it must be maintained! The fear of losing success once gained is greater than the fear of never reaching it.

While never succeeding can be blamed on a myriad of outside influences, the blame for squandering success generally sits on one's own shoulders. And nobody wants to take responsibility for that. It's easier to simply stay unhappy and be able to blame somebody else.

Blaming other people has become so "comforting" in our society (particularly here in the US). It has permeated many aspects of our culture, to almost comic effect (remember the person who was trying to sue McDonalds?). It drives me nuts.

Ladies and gentlemen, as adults, there is only one person responsible for your life, and that is you.

I cannot promise you will never meet another loser

again, but nobody makes you marry him (or her). Nobody makes you stay in an unhappy relationship. Nobody makes you accept lies or broken promises.

You have enormous power – but only if you choose to take the responsibility. Granted, there may be reasons why you feel the need to continue in an unhappy union: financial woes, young children, housing. But that is your CHOICE, for which you have sole responsibility.

There is always an alternative. Always, always, always. You do not have to stay. You do not have to say yes. I've gotten emails from people who are absolutely miserable in a marriage, tell me their partners won't go to counseling, won't try to work with them, but then also say their religious beliefs absolutely preclude divorce. Fair enough. But that is their choice.

I'm not here to make a judgment one way or another about why you do the things you do, only to say you always have a choice. And the choices you make have direct bearing on your success or failure in relationships. Of course, I also firmly believe being without a relationship is far more preferable to being within an unhappy one. But that's my choice.

It's scary to realize we have a choice. It's scary to think we're making choices about our lives every single day. It's frightening to realize we're that powerful. But we are. You are. With every choice you make, you impact the course of your life. So choose wisely.

8

○ STOP PICKING
AT IT!

Do you treat your relationship like a lab experiment?
Sadly, I think too many people do. Allow me to
explain.

It's probably not "politically correct" to do this
anymore, but years ago (when I was in high school) a
highlight of the biology curriculum was the actual
dissection of a frog. In the lab, students were paired
up at little dissecting tables with pins and scalpels,
and each pair was given a frog, which, until that
moment, had been quietly marinating in
formaldehyde.

We took our turns slicing, poking and prodding, and
what started out as a cute little amphibian always
ended up as an unrecognizable gelatinous blob.

Sadly, a consequence of our search for understanding was unfortunately destruction. Poor little froggy.

Recently, I received an email from a young woman in a newish relationship (funny, you don't look newish), who was going 'round and 'round in her head about her boyfriend, and what this comment meant, or whether she should have daily phone calls, or how often he should say "I love you" or whatever. I'm certain I'm not the only one with whom she shared these concerns. How much of her "unlimited night and weekend minutes" do you think were spent in deep thought and analysis on these issues? I'd say lots.

For every fleeting moment of pleasure we have in our relationships, we spend hours analyzing the meaning or ramifications. Every off-hand comment or forgotten pleasantry spawns days of analysis and examination. Grizzled, bearded scholars of Talmudic law don't spend as much time on their ancient Aramaic scriptures as we girls do on our boyfriends. And it's not pretty.

We poke and prod, and query and question until is it any wonder our cute little frog ends up a pile of mush?

Years ago when I was embarking on a new relationship, I got some great advice from a New Age-y sort of friend when I was doing some PhD-level analysis of my own. She told me to stop analyzing everything and just "BE." It was really hard at first. It meant letting go of a lot of habits and normal reference points I usually clung onto. It meant not second-guessing things and making assumptions. It was a little like flying and a little like falling, but most importantly, it allowed me to feel my feelings honestly. Do you know what I mean?

In other words, when it felt good, it was really good! Because my inner psyche wasn't constantly sitting in the wings, wondering about the ramifications of a kiss or a fun night out. It was just a great kiss or a terrific night out. There was no running commentary from the little voice in my head, making judgments or planting doubts.

And when something happened that bothered me, I was unencumbered by the usual "rules of engagement" – instead I could honestly say, "gee, that bothered me." I stopped looking around corners or waiting for the other shoe to drop and just purely experienced my feelings. It meant I stayed around for a much shorter time when the relationship was wrong and didn't mess it up when it was right.

Instead of spending so much time thinking about your relationship, spend more time simply feeling. Does this person make you feel good? Does this person make you feel bad? Do you feel good more than you feel bad?

The way you feel about someone must be based on the way you feel as a whole. Not based on one great weekend or one bad phone call. Relationships may be a collection of events, comments, days or moments, but the whole is much greater than the sum of the parts. If you poke it to bits, it will be unrecognizable and ultimately turn into a pile of guts.

After all, a pile of guts will never turn into a prince. But a frog just might.

9

HE DOESN'T NEED ANOTHER MOTHER

Isn't it interesting that only one letter changes "mother" to "smother"? I know the origin of these two words is unrelated in theory, but in practice, they can be like two peas in a pod.

Ladies, our unique ability to nurture, cosset and coddle is fundamental to the success of the human race. But it's the same ability that can destroy relationships.

It starts out innocently and lovingly enough. We meet a nice man. We want to impress him. We want to show him we care. So we do stuff for him. Take care of him. Buy him socks. Make his lunch. Anticipate his every need.

He loves it. We know he loves it, so we do it more. Pretty soon he stops buying his own socks. Never lifts a finger to make his own lunch. And we see him as helpless. So we fret over the socks and the lunch. My gawd! He has to live with holes in his socks. Oh no! He's going to starve because there is no lunch. We plan our schedules around the regular sock-buying and lunch-making. Our own socks have holes, and we go without lunch, but AT LEAST OUR MEN DON'T SUFFER!

And then, one morning we wake up and hate them for it. These helpless, wimpy, baby-men who can't even buy their own socks or slap together a sandwich without instructions. Hoo-boy, what losers. Where did they grow up? What sort of upbringing did they have to learn such useless behavior?

Uh…well…

You create a monster - you have to live with it. So don't create the monster to begin with. I know you love to do nice things and being kind and generous, but there's a big difference between doing nice things and doing everything.

To be sure, it's a tricky balance. But if you find yourself fretting over whether or not there will be something for him to eat when he comes home or planning your schedule around taking care of his laundry, or shopping, or meals, you're not being nice. You're slowly poisoning your relationship.

He's not your child. He's your partner. Your lover. But he won't be if you continue to take responsibility for his life.

Doing everything is emasculating. It turns you into the mother, and him into the son, and unless you have kinky tastes, it's a major passion-killer, believe you me.

No doubt there should be give and take in a relationship. Sometimes he takes care of you. Sometimes you take care of him. But if you're ALWAYS taking care of him, there is a serious imbalance. Is it any wonder you don't find him attractive any longer? Is it any wonder he argues with you over little things to establish some dominance?

I'm not saying it's all your fault. After all, he played along and allowed this situation to develop too. But I believe it's up to you to undo it.

He's a big boy. He's not going to starve if you don't pack a lunch for him. He's not that helpless. And if he is, what do you see in him anyway?

Back off a little bit. Let him be himself – the person you fell in love with initially. With the holey socks and fast food lunches. Resist the urge to remake him in your own image.

Changing your ingrained habits won't be easy. You'll probably meet some resistance, and you'll find it difficult to break your pattern. But start slowly. Just once a week, tell him he has to plan dinner. Chances are, you'll end up in a restaurant, but how bad is that? In any case, little by little you will undo the chain, and in the process re-discover some spontaneity and fun lurking in your relationship.

And if he throws a tantrum? Give him a good spanking and send him up to his room. Hmm, on second thought, he probably wouldn't view that as punishment. But seriously, if he throws a tantrum, you must stand your ground. Do not allow him to shovel guilt in your direction. Do not allow childlike pouting. Do not succumb to your mothering instinct. He'll get over it. And if he doesn't, you can get over him.

10

Nearly 20 years ago, when email and instant messaging were just a glint in some nerd's eye, I had a long-distance relationship. During a business conference, I met a very nice man who lived many thousands of miles away. After the conference, we wrote long letters to each other and talked on the telephone at least once a week. We planned trips to visit each other, and after a year, we made our long distance relationship very short distance. After all, that's generally the goal – to be as close together as possible, as often as possible.

Of course things have changed.

Now people have entire relationships – even affairs – online. I get emails from people who have initiated intimate relationships online, consummated them with "cyber sex" and then ended them when their online lovers became unfaithful! Long distance relationships are maintained for many months with constant real-time chats, frequent emails and of course, phone conversations.

For people who are unable to travel, are physically challenged, or located in some isolated spot, I can understand how a "virtual" online relationship can be a fulfilling alternative and certainly better than no relationship at all. Some people don't need a lot of contact with the object of their affection. Just knowing there is someone out there who cares, who sends emails and chats is enough. Or is it?

The thing is, although the way we are able to initiate and sustain a relationship (as a result of technology) has changed, we have not. Most of us still yearn for companionship, for emotional AND physical intimacy. And we need tangible proof now and then.

If you embark on a long-distance relationship, you must take all the issues of a close-proximity relationship and magnify them a hundred-fold. Trust. Fidelity. Honesty. If you think it's tough enough to believe your lover is faithful to you when he lives around the corner, imagine if he lived two states away.

In a long-distance relationship, you must truly believe the limited time you spend together is worth the trade-off of being apart for so much of the time. You must be willing to go home alone, night after night, until you and your lover are reunited.

Naturally, the reason many people are willing to accept the downside of a long distance relationship is because of the future upside – ultimately the long distance becomes very short distance. But this takes initiative and often some compromise – which is really what every successful relationship requires.

If your long-distance lover is only happy to see you when you travel there, you've got a one-way ticket to disappointment. You both need to make an effort, and unless you're happy with the relationship exactly as it is, one of these days, someone is going to have to get off the pot and move.

If your relationship started online, and that's the way your cyber honey wants to keep it, somebody is hiding something. Online you can be anything or anyone you want. For some, it's a great release. You can express virtual feelings and desires in relative anonymity, and try out different personas you wouldn't feel comfortable with in real life. But if you're both playing a role, who are you really in love with? Make sure you know who you're dealing with in the flesh. You need to be able to see eye-to-eye. Literally.

Phones, email and instant messaging can make long distances seem much closer. Online, the singles bars are open 24 hours a day, 365 days a year. "Geographically undesirable" is virtually meaningless. You have many more options to find the love of your life. But unless your relationship is built around those old fashioned qualities like honesty and commitment, you're always going to be miles and miles apart.

11

○ ARE YOU SURE
YOU WANT TO
WASTE TIME ON
AN AFFAIR?

I know a gal who is madly in love with a wonderful gorgeous man. She raves about the passion, the connection, the openness. According to this woman, she's simply never felt this sort of honest intimacy with any man, ever before. In fact, he has only one fault.

He's married.

Now I'm not one to judge the whys and wherefores of infidelity. From what I've learned, an affair is a symptom of a problem in the relationship, rather than the cause. I suppose there are examples where you thought you were happy with your current mate, and suddenly out of the blue, the most perfect person in the universe appears "across a crowded room, and somehow you know, you know even then" (thank you, Rogers and Hammerstein) that you are in deep love and must end your current relationship. But I think those thunderbolts are pretty few and far between.

No, what usually happens is boredom, or frustration, or resentment slowly permeates your relationship, almost invisibly, until you finally have a drink with that person you see at the gym all the time, and an arm around your waist becomes a kiss which becomes a caress and somehow you end up naked.

So you're either one of two main players: the adulterer, or the adulteree.

If you're the adulterer, the situation should alert you to a big issue. You're not happy in your relationship, for whatever reason, and something needs to be done. Either you work on your existing relationship, and fix the problem, or you end it.

If you're the adulteree, the situation should alert you to a different big issue. Your lover has a problem with honesty in relationships. He hasn't been honest with himself and what he's feeling, nor has he been honest with his wife and how he's feeling about her. So what makes you think he can possibly be honest with you?

Which is why I simply do not understand women (or men for that matter) who stay in affairs with married people for an extended period of time. Yes, it's exciting and the passion is great, and the clandestine nature of it adds excitement. But it's not a real, full, complete, honest relationship. So I guess if that's not what you want, then fine. Maybe you only need a day here and there to make you feel complete. Maybe you're also in another relationship and this affair just provides a supplement. It has worked that way in history. You marry for one reason or another. You mess around for fun.

But most people I've spoken to want more out of a relationship. And for some reason, women in particular seem willing to wait. And wait. Let me give you a piece of advice. Waiting around for your lover to make a decision gives him absolutely no incentive to change the situation. If he doesn't make any effort to get out of the relationship to be with you, he really doesn't want to get out of the relationship. He may have very noble reasons, but they do not make a clandestine affair noble.

You are being used. You provide a release for him. Like drinking, or drugs. But you're not helping him face reality or true honesty. What you need to do is tell him you love him, then tell him to call you when he's divorced. And then go shopping.

12

What is the definition of intimacy? A kiss? A canoodle? When you share secrets? When you pledge your troth? (When you actually know what that means?)

I think being married is a pretty intimate relationship. I think it's an agreement to share your life with someone, which means to share everything about your life together. Weelllll, maybe not EVERY little detail from the past - if it doesn't impact the present, it can probably stay tucked away in your mental archives. And I don't think you have to share every little thought you have in your head. But I certainly think it's reasonable to expect full disclosure on current actions and events.

I bring this up because a new bride was speaking to me about her husband, telling me about the work they've been doing on the family home and how they've been investing quite a bit in the improvements. Her husband has taken several months off in order to work full time on the house. The bride seemed to have some moderate concern about finances, and then mentioned her husband and father-in-law had purchased some property together, "But I'm not sure if they've sold it. I guess he'll tell me if he wants to."

Well, I don't know about you, but a red flag certainly appeared to me when she said that. This wasn't a business deal her husband was concerned with at work, but a personal deal that impacts the family finances. I think there needs to be full disclosure. I mean, what ELSE doesn't she know about?

Intimacy in a relationship, especially a marital relationship, means you share what happens in your life together. Not just social and sexual, but financial too. You need to be able to freely discuss your hopes, dreams and concerns. Above all, there should be no secrets.

How can you be truly intimate with someone, feel completely at one with them if you don't really know them, and know about them? I think total honesty is one of the most intimate expressions of love we have. It's the most naked we can be.

When nothing comes between us and our partners -

no secrets, half-truths or lies – we can feel comfortable, secure and free. It's the wonderful by-product of trust. If you're always wondering what might be around the corner, what surprises may be lurking, you can never relax. Never truly allow yourself to fall freely into love.

If you have questions about your partner, his or her activities or actions, you must be able to ask about them, and discuss them openly. If that's not possible in your relationship, it's a really big red flag. Not a good sign. Because whatever is left unsaid and unaddressed will fester. Like a big ugly pimple.
If I've said it once, I've said it a gazillion times: communication is the key to a healthy relationship. If you're afraid to ask something because you're afraid of the answer, that's your first big clue there's something amiss. You probably already know the truth.

13

Ah, the cozy comfort of a stable relationship. Always having someone to cuddle up with. Friday nights with a pizza and movie, curled up on the sofa. Leisurely Sunday breakfast with a big stack of newspapers and a bigger stack of pancakes. No need to go out on a Saturday night trawling, because you've already hauled in your catch. Oh, the contentment. And...the...boredom.

I often say that everything in life is a trade-off, and in terms of relationships, you trade the often stressful excitement of dating for warm and fuzzy stability. Which unfortunately can turn into dull monotony. That forces a break-up. And generates more stressful excitement.

The conundrum is that most of us do really crave a stable relationship. We actually work hard to build the sort of thing we end up running screaming from years or even months later.

If only we could keep the comfort and ban the boredom.

So how do you do it? Well, here's what not to do.

1. Don't close yourself off to the rest of the world. One of the things that makes you interesting to your partner is the fact that you have other interests. So don't stop doing the things that made you YOU before you became a WE. If you used to play sports or throw pottery, make time for those other activities (unless you used to be a lap dancer unless your partner wants to come along and watch).

2. Don't stop being spontaneous. That's what makes dating so fun! You never know what you're going to do next weekend. So why not give each other the "assignment" of planning a night out. One Friday it's your responsibility, the next, your sweetie's. Don't let them tell you what's up until the last minute.

3. Don't be afraid to be a teeny bit kinky. Turn off the tv one night and play strip poker, or strip Parcheesi. It doesn't matter! Make time for each other and play a game. Have a massage night or a "9 1/2 Weeks Night." Take a bunch

of things out of the fridge, take turns blindfolding each other and see if you can guess what you're tasting or touching. It may make you think twice about eating Miracle Whip...

4.   Don't stop trying to make an impression. Remember when you went out on a date, and you spent hours agonizing over what to wear, and then the special ritual you went through to get all dolled up? A friend of mine calls it going for a "full poodle." Well, don't forget your "doggy style." Woof woof. Keep dressing up for each other. Yes, those Swiss cheese sweats may be the most comfortable garments on the planet, but they are NOT alluring.

The thing is: fighting boredom does take some effort. Because that's really what caused boredom in the first place – the lack of effort. So keep trying! The excitement really is still there, buried under the sofa pillows, TV Guide, sweat pants and Doritos bags. Trust me. You just have to dig it out.

14

○ IT'S OKAY TO
TAKE A BREAK

Gimme a break! As spokeschick for an entire gender, I'd like to lobby for relationship "days off." Not to misbehave, just to have "single" days now and then. In all other aspects of our lives, we get days off. We don't have to work 7 days a week, we don't have to go to the gym every single day. We don't go to church every day. Parents get breaks from their kids when they call the babysitter. And I'd like to have the same for my relationship (except for the babysitter part).

Every once in awhile I'd like to go back to those selfish "me" days when I didn't need to worry what someone else wanted to do, or have to be back at a certain time to make dinner, or take care of someone else's laundry. Granted, I'm very lucky in my relationship. We're pretty evenly split on all the chores, and my sweetie in no way imposes. But every once in awhile, I think back to those pre-sweetie Friday nights when I'd come home, read the paper and fall asleep in front of the tv. Didn't have to think about making dinner, or being entertaining or sexy. Just taking a little time out.

There's nothing "sinister" about my desire. There's no one else I want to be with. I don't want to be running out with the girls and staying out until 3 am (I think I'm waaaay too old for that stuff now). It's just the "individual" time I miss. Where I could be all by myself and not feel like I'm ignoring someone.

I feel responsibility in the relationship to be a good partner when we're together. I want to be "there" and "present." And that does take effort. It's just that sometimes I kinda like being totally alone, responsible only to myself, making decisions just for myself.

In "Men Are From Mars, Women Are From Venus," John Gray talks about men needing to go "in their caves" from time to time. I suppose I'd like the same for women, except my cave would be stocked with a cosmetics counter I can browse through at my leisure, a few packages of Pepperidge Farm Milanos and a stack of magazines.

The problem is: it's tricky expressing this need to your partner without sounding negative. How do you tell someone you want to be alone without appearing that you don't want to be with them? The truth is, you'll love being with them even more after the little break, but not everyone will be so sure!

As with everything in a relationship, it comes down to communication. When you communicate openly about your love and feelings, you build up the trust and confidence to discuss your needs. I suppose I don't need to be physically alone, just "left alone" to putter around in my girlie way, on my own girlie schedule. And I'll bet if I discussed this with my honey, he'd be overjoyed to have a "manly" day too, where he could putter with his tool kit out in the garage, wear smelly clothes, eat nachos with that horrible plastic yellow cheese sauce and fart with abandon. In fact I'm going to try it! (Not the farting part, the discussion part.)

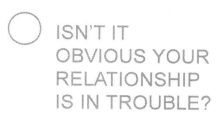

15

A relationship generally doesn't go bad overnight. Even if something happens all at once to trigger a problem or break-up, chances are it was festering quietly under the surface before erupting. And even before the festering stage, there was a slow decline, a downshifting from the way it "used to be." It's almost imperceptible, which makes it all the more insidious. You don't even notice things are going downhill. It makes it easier to accept the change, because it happens little by little. You get into new routines which seem "normal" and then the decline continues.

But the secret to a long, happy and successful relationship is making sure you address the concerns long before they have a chance to incubate. So how do you find out you have a problem if you don't know you have a problem? I believe there are little warning signs, little innocuous things that point to some level of dissatisfaction within your relationship. The root could be in you, it could be with your partner, or it could be external. I'm not here to interpret that. Only to say, if you notice any of the following early warning signs, it may be time to stop and think about your relationship and what's affecting it.

Sexy dreams about someone else – Once every now and then is one thing, but if it begins to happen too often (like every week), I think it's your subconscious fishing for new stimulation. Dreams are "safer" places than fantasies because you're not consciously making an effort.

Enjoying being by yourself more and more – We all need "me" time, and everyone has varying degrees of that need. But if the need changes significantly and you find you'd really rather prefer to do stuff by yourself – especially things you used to enjoy doing with your partner – it could be a sign that something's amiss.

Wanting to be out with your buddies – This is the flipside of the one above. Remember when you first got together with your beloved? Your friends thought you'd abandoned them. But now, you find you'd rather be out with them, or at least out with other people when you're with your partner. It's just not fun if it's just the two of you. Red flag!

Irritation over small things that didn't irritate before – Nobody's perfect (not even moi). We all have little peccadilloes (I'm resisting the urge to make a rude comment), and when the relationship is shiny and new, we graciously overlook them. We may continue to overlook them forever. Or they may become a flashpoint for little arguments. Those little piles of socks and underwear used to be endearing, until one day, they become an affront to nature. What happened? They're still the same socks. Time to do a bit of analysis.

Not looking forward to bedtime – If you happily cohabitate, I think you'll agree that end of the day cuddling is one of the high points of the day. Even if it doesn't lead to canoodling, cuddling is generally a nice thing. But if you find yourself thinking of other things to do rather than meet your partner under the covers, you've got some thinking to do!

Realizing you haven't spontaneously said "I love you" in awhile – It used to trip off your tongue easily. In fact, you may have blurted it out once or twice at most inopportune times. But now you hardly say it. You think you're feeling it, but somehow it never makes it past your lips. I certainly hope you're taking your sweetie for granted. Or is it something else...?

So that's my little list. If any of these sounds familiar, it doesn't mean your relationship is headed for a break-up; it just means there might be some things you need to address BEFORE it gets ugly and hairy.

16

○ GIVE MEN
   WHAT THEY
   WANT – NOW
   AND THEN

Okay, here's my free bonus earth-shattering pronouncement: men and women are different.

I know this sounds blatantly obvious, but I'm afraid we often forget. In our (culturally recent) desire to institute measures of equality in many aspects of our society, we have also tried to force equality or uniformity in emotional or sexual expression.

The fact is: men and women respond differently. Before you get all hot and bothered and tell me I'm generalizing, let me agree. Yes, it is a generalization, and I know there is also considerable variance along the respective continuums (continua?) for each gender. (Ooh, "continua" – now there's a two-dollar word. By the way, according to Webster, they're both acceptable. But I digress).

In any case, we need to get over it. Accept the difference and stop fighting it. After all, it makes the world go 'round.

So gals, to help you enhance your relationships with your men, I'd like to discuss not what WE want, but what THEY do.

I'll say it once again, slowly: guys are very visual. Whereas we like to hear sweet nothings, they want us to wear them.

I was reminded of this over the weekend. My sweetie and I were getting ready to go out. I was dressed, wearing a skirt, and he asked if I was wearing underwear. I said yes, a thong. He said, "Really! Have I seen it before?" I said, "No, I don't think so. Would you like to?" Of course he replied, "Why not!" Well I can assure you, when I have a new blouse or handbag, it does not pique his interest (or anything else for that matter). But he definitely takes an interest in my lingerie. And I, for one, am glad!

To be honest, sometimes I'd prefer NOT wearing scratchy lace things and uncomfortable high heels, or I've got period bloat or a bad hair day. But when I get dolled up for my man, and he responds, all of a sudden I feel like a sex kitten. It works for both of us.

I can already hear the angry email heckling. It's the objectification of women! Yeah, right, but what does he ever do to seduce me! Why can't he get excited by me in sweats – that's all I ever get from him! After the baby throws up on me for the third time, you think I can even THINK about lace bras?

Well, let me address these points. First of all, I'm not talking about parading in front of a paying audience – just an audience of one: your lover. And I'm not talking about anything degrading – simply about enhancing your femininity and giving pleasure to your partner. Why wouldn't you want to do that?

There will indeed be days when you don't feel like it, and he will have to understand. Just as there will be days when he doesn't feel like giving you a neck rub. But ladies, we need to understand it's important to our men. They like the visual stimulation. They like the high heels, and the cleavage, and the lace. Let's oblige, now and then.

If you can't get what you want from HIM, it's not the fault of the stilettos; it's your relationship. And if I've said it once, I've said it a gazillion times, the only way to fix that, is to talk about it. Withholding your Victoria's Secret collection will not fix a problem. It will create new ones.

So, just in case you're thinking ahead for gift giving, I shall close with a suggestion. You know what your man would really love in his Christmas stockings this year? You. Wearing them. Preferably with heels.

17

○ YES YOU **DO**
HAVE A CHOICE.
IN FACT YOU
HAVE THREE

Do you have a nose on your face? Well that's very handy (or nosey, I suppose).

The reason I ask is I get a lot of emails from people asking for advice on relationships and marriages, and what to do when there's a problem. People are looking for help and guidance with predicaments such as "my husband doesn't want sex with me anymore" or "I'm unhappy with my boyfriend" or even "I hate my job."

Well I have good news. Although the specific action points for each of these may be different, the choices you have are not only consistent, but as plain as the nose on your face (and we've already established you do indeed have one).

Whenever there is something in your life you're not happy about, you ALWAYS have these three choices:

1. Find out how to fix it.
2. Keep it exactly the same.
3. Do something completely different.

The great thing is if one doesn't work, you can always try another. For example, "my husband doesn't want sex with me anymore." Well, the first thing to do is find out how to fix it. Speak with your husband and find out what he's feeling and what makes him feel that way. Maybe he isn't able to talk to you about it, because it has to do with how he feels about you. Perhaps he would consider counseling. Maybe it's a medical problem and he needs to see a doctor. Or maybe it's something you can solve together with better communication, which makes the problem magically disappear.

But perhaps there is an impasse. He won't talk about it. You can't change what's bothering him. No matter what, a solution is impossible. If that's the situation, you must consider your second choice, which is keeping everything exactly the same.

After all, you've been together all these years. If you still love each other, there are many other great things you share – sex just isn't one of them. As I always (and I do mean always) say, everything in life is a trade-off. Perhaps it simply makes more sense, from a financial, business, or family perspective to just stay together. If that's the choice you make, you should ultimately feel resolution and contentment. You've thought about it carefully, and that's what makes the most sense.

But maybe it doesn't. Maybe you can't bear to keep things the same. Your husband won't talk to you about it. You've gone to counseling by yourself and it hasn't helped. You can't stand the thought of staying in this loveless marriage for another 15 years – let alone even one. In which case you must consider your final choice: doing something completely different. Perhaps it's time to move on.

The issue most people have with solving problems is not that they don't understand the choices they have, but rather they are unable or afraid to act.

I am certain you go through the three obvious choices in your head, but when you come to what you know is the correct answer – and it's not the easy answer you want – you go around again and end up going in circles. Around and around, unable to sleep, unable to think about anything else or do anything about it. The problem is deep inside you know the answer. That itching, burning sensation isn't hemorrhoids, but the truth, itching and burning to get out.

So you know what you do instead? You complain. Complaining is very useful – but not for what you think. Complaining does not relieve the problem, or make it go away. The desire to complain is your gut's way of reminding you something needs to change, that you need to take action. And just in case you missed it the first time, I will remind you of your three choices:

1. Find out how to fix it (so you have no reason to complain).
2. Keep it exactly the same (accept your fate and stop complaining).
3. Do something completely different (remove the source of your complaint).

Remember, with each problem or challenge that comes your way, you ALWAYS have choices. Even if you always elect to keep everything exactly the same, go through the process of evaluating the pros and cons of each choice so you understand and accept why you're not going to do anything about it. Then immediately stop beating yourself up about it, and move on with your life. And most importantly, stop complaining.

18

They say an elephant never forgets, but I wonder if it
ever forgives?

No doubt, some crappy stuff has happened to you
and yours in the last 12 months – it's very difficult to
have a crap-free year. I know many folks who are still
brushing off the effects of natural disasters. And I
know many more of you have had to deal with
UNnatural disasters as well – those of an emotional
kind.

A disaster like this may not shake the earth, but it will
rock your world, causing a seismic shift in your heart
and potentially irreparable damage. So how do you
get over it? How do you move ahead into the future
without dragging a semi-truck full of crap from the
past?

Well, first of all, I'm with the elephants. I don't think you should ever forget. You can't learn if you never remember.

Remember sharp knives cut fingers as easily as tomatoes. Remember the burner on the stove stays hot for a long time. Remember your car won't move if the needle gets to "E." Remember that load of BS you believed despite all the red flags. Remember how you said you wouldn't go back after the first time it happened.

You need to remember. You need to remember things aren't always what they seem and there are no guarantees. You need to remember if things seem too good to be true, they generally are.

To move on, it is not necessary to forget. In fact, I don't recommend it at all– unless you're happy to go through the same experience again and again. You must NOT forget, if you want to learn from experience. But that doesn't mean you should think about it over and over again, and beat yourself up until there's nothing left of you but a squishy blob of regret and heartache.

To truly move ahead, you must forgive. Not because the other person deserves it, but because YOU do. In "The Four Agreements," Don Miguel Ruiz says sometimes the offending party doesn't really deserve forgiveness. But you certainly do.

You deserve to be free of the sadness and anger and

hurt. You deserve to move ahead, learn from your mistakes and seek new happiness, a better happiness, based on honesty and reality. Will you ever be the same again? No. Will your partner be? No. Will your relationship be? No. Would you want it to be? HECK no!

You don't want to go back to the way it was. The way it was got you into the mess you're in! You need to go forward to the way it SHOULD be. And that is why you must forgive, so you can move forward.

Let it go. It happened. Get over it. If you don't get over it, you are allowing the "villain" to hurt you over and over again. You give that person far greater power than they ever had to begin with! They may have hurt you in the past, but why should you let that same event hurt you again and again in the future?

You must move on. You must also bear in mind that nothing will ever be the same. You will never be the same. The relationship will never be the same. But read my lips (okay, read my words): You don't want it to be.

You don't want the same old relationship, with the same old hurt and lies. You want the new and improved, non-stick, fresher-smelling model.

Which reminds me of a riddle. If an elephant didn't have a trunk, how would he smell? My friends, trunk or no trunk, he'd still smell like an elephant.

THE SEX PART

1

WHEN IT
COMES TO
LIBIDO, SIZE
MATTERS

How important is sex to you? In your list of must-
haves in life, where does sex rank? Is it in the top
three? The top ten? Or does it fall somewhere
between "self-cleaning oven" and "HBO?"

Awhile back I was talking to a young man about his
relationship. He told me he loved his girlfriend very
much, but she was hardly interested in sex. Whereas
he could make love to her for hours, she would
complain he was taking too long. As a consequence,
he found his eyes wandering to other women, and his
brain (both upper and lower) often overheated.

He asked me if I thought sex was important in a
relationship, and I resisted all temptation to scream
back at him, at the top of my lungs, "Are you f***ing

NUTS?" Instead I said, "Why, yes."

Of COURSE sex is important - assuming your relationship is non-platonic and between two consenting adults. But it doesn't matter if it's once a month or once a day. It doesn't matter if you need a special chair or a trapeze or elaborate costumes. It matters not if you like it with the lights on, or the lights off, or via flashlight.

What does matter is that you and your partner like it about the same. Or so it seems to me. But maybe I'm crazy.

Recently I went to one of the popular online matchmaking sites and submitted myself to the personality questionnaire. I was curious to see how much sex figured into the profile. Out of easily three hundred qualities I was asked to input, about 10 had to do with sex – and mostly in vague terms. That's only about 3%. THREE percent! According to this site, 97% of your relationship has to do with something other than sex.

I will agree there are other factors MORE important than sex. And I will also agree that the relative importance of sex changes in your relationship over time. The amount, type and frequency of physical intimacy you and your partner require is incredibly personal. It's a delicate balance you work out together and adjust as necessary. But hell's bells! It's more than THREE percent of your relationship, isn't it???

When you're mismatched in that area, when either of you is dissatisfied, I promise you the importance is going to be a whole heckuva lot more than three percent.

The key is compatibility: finding someone with the same level of passion, the same preferences. If you share 97% of your qualities but don't share the same interest in sex, I think you share a big problem. UNLESS one of you is willing to compromise.

But how do you do that? In the case of my young friend, how is he supposed to suppress his raging hormones? Run to the bathroom with a magazine after every night out? And what of his girlfriend? Is she supposed to submit to his advances and let him have his way simply to keep peace in the relationship? Perhaps they'll find a compromise that works. But I'm not putting any money on it.

If you enjoy sex and want sex to be an ongoing part of your relationship, I firmly believe you must share "intrinsic" attraction with your partner and an equal desire for sex from the very beginning. The novelty and excitement is bound to diminish over time. It may be replaced with something else like deeper love, but if you were never really that physically attracted to your partner in the first place, it's highly unlikely attraction will suddenly appear down the road.

Age, illness, disabilities, pregnancy, stress, fatigue – there are many things that will affect and change our desire and ability for sex throughout our lives. But at least if you begin on the same level playing field, with an equal, compatible interest in sex, you will be better equipped to adapt as times goes on. And I'm 97% sure of that.

2

A friend of mine recently told me about an issue with her "booty call." For the (few) uninitiated, let me first define this terminology as follows: a "booty call" is someone with whom you have semi-regular, quite casual sex. This is most often done very, very late at night after the bars have closed, when you're not quite ready to go home and everything seems like a good idea. To commence a booty call, you must first make a "booty call" on the cell phone (either text or voice) to your appointed candidate. The actual discussion/negotiation for the activity is conducted in thinly veiled code, and the exchange will go something like this:

a.	Hey.
b.	Hey.
a.	You home now?
b.	Yeah.
a.	Can I come over?
b.	Yeah.
a.	K. Bye.

Now in theory, a booty call seems like quite an excellent arrangement. You get fairly decent regular sex, without all the icky trappings of a relationship.

In theory.

I return now to my friend, and her booty call concern.

She and her "booty call" had been enjoying each other's charms as regularly as each had both desired, and all was well. They would occasionally see each other at the local bar for some very casual conversation, and all was well. Then one night, my friend sees her "booty call" at the bar with another woman. Now, on the surface this is not actually a violation of booty call terms. After all, under the terms of a booty call, neither party has made any commitment of monogamy to the other. It's just sex, right? But here's the problem. My friend's booty call was actually being AFFECTIONATE with the other woman, hissing her and appearing to administer tenderness. In front of my friend! All was no longer well.

But why not? It was just a booty call, right? Ah, but

for booty callers and call-ees, the unspoken agreement in effect states, "I can accept that you use me as a vessel for your sexual release as long as that's how you treat everyone else too."

The thing about sharing sexual intimacy with someone is that after a one-night stand, it is transformed into something more. No way to avoid it.

A one-night stand is just for one night. You get your rocks off; I get my rocks off and we never see each other again. Period. There is no such thing as a two-night stand. Or three weekends in a row stand. Or every Thursday after the game stand. Anything more than one night of casual sex, and scary things start to rear their ugly heads. Things like respect and caring and attachment (let alone the accidental creation of a life). I simply don't believe it's possible to have sex whenever you want with no strings attached. There are always strings dangling out there. After all, there is no such thing as a free lunch. Why should a robust shag be any different?

Sooner or later, one of the parties involved is going to say, "Waaaaaaait a minute, I thought you were MY special friend. I'm not so comfortable sharing you with HER."

In theory, it would be delightful to have the option of familiar, reliable sex via a booty call. But for most people, I don't believe it can be done entirely without the need for respect or ultimately, emotional connection.

And by the way, if for some reason you ARE able to maintain a long-term booty call completely free of all respect and emotional involvement, what does that say about you?

3

R YOU SURE YOU NEED THE TOYS?

The human body is rather ingeniously designed for sex, don't you think? First of all, it's covered with sensitive skin, which (depending on your particular cleansing, toning and moisturizing regimen) is also delightful to touch. Bodies also feature a variety of peaks and valleys attractively packaged in appealing shapes which produce wonderful, pleasurable sensations for both the toucher and the touchee. And if all that weren't enough, bodies also come with a variety of "stimulation tools" including fingers, toes, a tongue and specialized accoutrements depending on gender, which can provide a broad range of sensations and experiences.

I'll be honest with you. My human body has done a pretty darn good job of providing me with delightful sexual experience over the last few decades. And if I may say so, it seems to have done the trick when I haven't been alone either. I gotta tell you. I'm STILL not bored. None of my stones have been left unturned.

But after a discussion with some friends over the weekend, I began to think that perhaps I'm abnormal. Or a throwback. A "Luddite" for the sexual revolution. You see, I eschew technology.

I may well be in the minority. In my informal sample of friends, probably about 50% had employed or regularly employ the services of "novelties." They were able to converse knowledgably about rabbit pearls, swings, G-spot worms, butterflies, pulsators and "Bobbi Sue."

I will admit an experience with a neck massager some years ago that found its way further south, but it's not something I've had any desire to repeat. I mean, sex is a natural organic process. After all, its primary reason for being is the creation of life, not sales for Duracell.

Of course, we humans enjoy sexual activity far more as recreation than procreation, which is fab. Other than perhaps shopping, there are few activities more wonderful than rolling around with another warm body, giving and receiving pure pleasure.

But I want to do it with a nice warm BODY, not an appliance! I mean, I really, really love my food processor, but I wouldn't want to go to bed with it.

Is sex without equipment really that boring? Are we so clumsy at providing pleasure for our partners that we must resort to twitching lumps of latex to do the trick?

I sometimes think the proliferation of sex toys and aids mirrors the rise of other "convenience" devices in our society. We look to technology to solve every problem, eliminate every unwanted chore. Why talk to your partner about what really gives them pleasure (and risk hearing the answer) when you can push a button and get results.

Rather than increasing intimacy, I wonder if sex toys reduce it. Where's the intimate knowledge, the love, the generosity in flipping the switch on the "Impulse Gyrating Beaded Dolphin" (only $79.95, with 6 levels of gyration, an ultra-powerful clitoral stimulator with an incredible 7 patterns of vibration, pulsation, & escalation, and 40 heavy-duty rotating metal beads in synchronized, non-jamming rows)?

OR is it so difficult to achieve pleasure that we really must have help? Maybe I'm completely wrong about our ingenious design. Perhaps it's not so perfect after all. Maybe for most of us an orgasm is a vague, unattainable concept unless we have some battery-operated assistance.

OR should we blame the media for telling us that multiple screaming orgasms are our birthright? Have we come to believe that the only good sex is a several hour marathon of sweaty pleasure?

I will tell you one thing for sure. I get hundreds of emails from people all over the world who have problems with their relationships. You know what's the biggest problem people have? The root of so much unhappiness? Communication. They can't talk to each other. They don't know how to ask. They don't know how to express their feelings.

Everybody is different – every BODY is different. Hey, whatever floats your boat. If your tastes run to cherry-scented latex and pulsating, strap-on farm animals, go ahead, bust a moooove.

But before you run out to your neighborhood novelty emporium to find the solution to your unsatisfied desires, first shut the curtains, turn the lights down low, and try something very intimate with your partner. It can be very satisfying whether you're naked or fully clothed, but the main thing is you both have to be into it. I'll give you a hint– it's a four letter word and it ends with "k."

TALK.

Have you ever actually told each other where you like to be touched? And how? Have you ever pointed out the exact spots that are hot-wired to your "oh yes!" nerve? Have you ever asked for what you want?

Ultimately, it's about making each other feel good –

however that may be. I may be the lone voice in the crowd, but I think with good, intimate communication and a little bit of trial and error, we can figure out a way together to make the fireworks fly.

After all, I'm quite certain my honey would prefer me to get all hot and bothered thinking about the way his special parts touch my special parts, rather than me excitedly anticipating the hum of "the uniquely shaped three-color jelly "Luscious Lollipopper" with flexible stem to massage and probe."

4

○ PORN AIN'T THE NORM

The naked human form is one of the most celebrated subjects of art. As long as we homo sapiens have been scratching pictures on cave walls, we've been doodling nudies. After all, we've got sex on the mind a lot of the time. Our success as a species depends on it, and besides, it's fun.

So we like to look at paintings, and photos and videos of people doing it. We read books and magazines about people doing it. We make up jokes about people doing it. We sing songs about it.

The history and litany of erotic art and literature is long and deep (no pun intended). Erotica is studied and appreciated. We might even call it "tasteful." In fact, the definition of erotic is "devoted to, or tending to arouse sexual love or desire." Love and desire. Tasteful indeed.

Then there's pornography.

The origin of pornography is "pornographos" - writing about prostitutes. Rather than love and desire, the dictionary says pornography depicts behavior intended to cause sexual excitement.

Now, sexual excitement between two people (adults, and two HUMAN people, not one human and one farm animal) who already love and desire each other is a fine thing. Many people find a little pornography to be just the thing to get the juices flowing. You get interesting ideas about new things to try. It helps spice up the regular routine.

 Personally, my tastes run to the more "erotic" - especially if you consider a great meal and lovely bottle of wine under that heading. But who am I to judge?

Well, you know me...I never pass up an opportunity to pass judgment. And in this particular instance, I've been invited to.

I've gotten many emails from women who say their husbands and boyfriends are obsessed by pornography. The women say their men spend hours and hours on their computers, viewing pornographic material. Not material that generates "love and desire" for their wives and girlfriends, but sexual excitement. Alone.

The men say there's nothing wrong with it. The women aren't so sure.

Well ladies, you're right.

As I've mentioned before, in general men are more stimulated visually than are women. That's why you notice them staring at other women. And why they enjoy "Fear Factor Models" so much, and cheerleaders. And why they not only like to look at the Victoria's Secret catalogue, but also want to see you wearing something from it. All that is normal.

But staying tucked away, in a darkened room, staring at writhing, slippery bodies on the computer for hours at a time is a symptom of a larger problem.

Here are some other symptoms. The two of you find it difficult to have an intimate conversation. When you do have sex (which isn't often), it's over in a flash, and probably only one of you is satisfied. You don't go out and do anything fun anymore. He says there's no problem, but he seems to barely know you're there.

The porn isn't the problem. It's the relationship.

Something has happened in your relationship or in his life that makes watching porn alone a desirable alternative to reality. It could be many things - and not all of them have to do with sex or sexual repression. It could have something to do with how your relationship has evolved over the years.

The roles we play and the way we view our partners often changes over the years – so gradually, we don't see it, until one day we finally wake up and discover we're not with the same person we started with. We're probably not the same either.

For whatever reason, the intimacy between the two of you is gone. Obsessively viewing pornography takes the place of that intimacy and prevents you from connecting together. But for that matter, obsessively doing ANYthing to the point of excluding those close to you is a problem.

The only way to fix it is to start talking. And that's the hard part. Because if you're having trouble baring yourselves to each other physically, imagine how difficult it will be baring your innermost soul. But that's the only way to move forward.

Talk with each other or with a counselor. And if he won't go with you, go by yourself. Because if the only place he's comfortable is in a darkened room by himself, you might have to leave him there for good.

5

○ STRIP CLUBS AREN'T NORMAL EITHER, NO MATTER WHAT HE SAYS

I'd like to ask men a question. What's the big deal with strip clubs? Why would anyone want to visit them more than once in a very blue moon? I guess the "show" is fairly entertaining, the first time you attend. Seeing lovely people dance in skimpy clothing is pleasant indeed – why they've been doing it in the ballet for hundreds of years. Similarly, it's aesthetically pleasing to watch belly dancers shimmy, and scantily clad showgirls bounce around glitzy extravaganzas in Las Vegas. But the purpose of these entertainments is not (at least not overtly) to incite sexual stimulation. It's just nice to look at.

Of course, I suppose that's what most of you would say about nubile females writhing in your lap, wearing nothing more than heavy eye makeup, a G-string and platform shoes.

Yeah, right.

I've met many men who regularly attend strip clubs, men who are eager to purchase horribly overpriced beverages and stuff dollar bills into some stranger's sweaty underpants while their friends and strangers goad them on. I think it's akin to prostitution. It's the oldest profession in the world. There will always be a market for it (just as there will always be someone who actually WANTS to eat White Castle "sliders"). But my question (just as it is for the sliders), is why would you want to? What makes you need it?

So, here's my theory as to why a man regularly goes to a strip club (I'm not talking about once or twice, just to see what it's like, I'm talking regularly):

1.   He's not getting any. Maybe he's just out of a relationship. Maybe he's never had a relationship. Maybe he's in the armed forces and getting any is out of the question. So for all you lonely guys out there, I understand and hope it's just a temporary situation. But if this is the only kind of "relationship" you can have with a woman, you've got some issues. Get some help.

2.   He's not getting what he wants from his partner. This is a HUGE relationship issue, and I suppose going to a strip club is "better" than having an affair, but it stems from the same thing. If you need more than you're

getting from your partner right now, you need to talk to her about it. Now.

3. He's a bit of a perv. It's just weird to only ever want to watch.

And speaking of watching, I'd like to put in my two cents about pornography. First of all, I'd like to differentiate between "pornography" and what I'd prefer to call "erotica." To me, erotica is sexually explicit material between consenting adults. Pornography is everything else. And frankly, I'd rather not know it exists.

Erotica, on the other hand, has had a place in our society since there was society. It is celebrated in art and literature, and it takes many forms of expression. I suppose lap dancing is one of those forms.

Many people enjoy erotica and find it adds a vivid dimension to their lovemaking. But I'll be honest, I'd rather not watch someone else doing it. I want to do it myself! In an intimate, loving relationship, the "regular" stuff is still pretty darn fun. I look forward to never "needing" outside stimulation, toys or paraphernalia to keep the glint in my eye. Maybe I'm being idealistic, but that's what I think my sweetie is for. And that's why I think there's something "odd" about men who look forward to watching some detached stranger go through the motions. How can that ever be better than the real thing?

6

YOUR SEX PROBLEMS ARE SYMPTOMS

The turn of the last century was not a particularly great time to be a canary. In the early 1900's, the little yellow birds were used to detect odorless poisonous gas in coalmines. After a mine fire or explosion, rescuers would descend into the mine carrying a canary in a small cage. If Tweetie keeled over, conditions were unsafe, and the rescuers made a hasty return to the surface (which I suppose made it sort of a bummer not only for the bird, but the miners left behind).

In any case, miners knew the problem was not with the canary, but the coalmine.

Which brings me to your sex life. (And if that's not a literary stretch, I don't know what is. Okay. I do know what is: the next sentence.)

My friends, your sex organs are the canaries of your coalmines.

If you can't get your canary to tweet anymore, it ain't the bird's fault. The problem lies somewhere deeper. I'll put it another way. If the cookies taste like crap, don't blame the oven.

In fact, I'll go out on a limb here and estimate that approximately 83.6% of all sex problems have nothing to do with sexual anatomy at all.

That is not to say that certain physical problems can and do affect performance. Fatigue, illness, aging, and hormonal changes can all quench fires.

But if you can't find that spark, most likely it's not that you're feeling too little passion. Instead, you may be feeling way too much of something else. Sadness. Insecurity. Stress. Frustration. Anger. Guilt. Fear.

What you're feeling inside emotionally has enormous effect on what you're feeling sexually. Your desire, response and pleasure are all intimately related to what's in your head.

And until you address the emotional issues you may have with your partner (or perhaps most importantly, with yourself), you cannot solve the sexual issues. You must get to the underlying cause to solve the problem.

When you have a cold, you have certain symptoms: headache, stuffy nose, cough. There are lots of products you can take to make yourself feel better for the moment, but the fact is, you still have a cold. And until you get rid of the cold, you won't be healthy again.

If your polar ice caps aren't melting or your flag is always at half-mast, don't ask yourself "why don't I feel anything?" Instead ask "WHAT am I feeling?" And then get out one of the most effective sexual aids I know:

A pen and paper.

First, make a list of all the adjectives describing how you feel at that moment. Angry. Irritated. Bored. Uninterested. Hurt. Disappointed. Whatever it is.

Then, after every adjective, write "because" and fill in the blank. In other words, "Bored - because he doesn't try like he used to." "Hurt - because we always have to do what she wants."

The last step is to write "which means" after every phrase, and then fill in the final blank. In other words, "Bored – because he doesn't try like he used to – which means - he doesn't care about me any more" or "Hurt – because we always have to do what she wants – which means – I always feel weak and powerless."

Once you've identified what you're feeling and what's causing it, you can start to fix it. That's the good news. The bad news is it probably won't be an instant fix. You're probably going to have to talk about it. A lot. You may have to change your behavior, or ask someone else to change theirs.

But just like weight loss or fitness, there is no instant fix. It will take some effort. Sometimes simply understanding is effort enough, but more often than not, you'll need to change some habits, change the way you react, and possibly accept a new reality.

If your canary is sick, there's trouble at the mine. You're not going to fix it by getting a new canary.

7

MAYBE YOU SHOULD SAY NO

Yes! Yes! Yes! That wonderful moment when you surrender to unbridled passion and open your arms (or whatever) to sex. You know when it's right.

Pretty much.

Most of the time.

Or do you? Do you know when it's wrong? When you might be better off saying, "Gosh, thanks but no thanks." When the best response might be to walk briskly in the opposite direction. When it might be a good idea to think ahead and consider the implications of the next 10 minutes or so. (Some of you are thinking TEN minutes! Wow. An athlete.)

But do you really know when it's okay to say no? Or even, when you MUST say no? I think we put too much emphasis on saying yes, rather than putting a little thought against why throwing caution to the wind, having a little fling and saying what the heck might not be such a good idea after all. Cool your jets, and turn down your afterburners if any of the following apply:

1. **It doesn't feel right.** The way I look at it, sex is supposed to feel good. Now perhaps that viewpoint is too "conventional," but that's my opinion. Feeling good and sex should go hand in hand (or wherever you prefer). If you ever get into a situation where it doesn't feel good or right, or even the IDEA of it doesn't feel good, don't do it. Say no. Politely, of course. Firmly, if need be. But "no" just the same.

    Yes, we're all supposed to be unselfish, giving lovers, but that assumes we want to be doing it in the first place. Better to say no, than go through the motions, fake enjoyment or communicate disgust. The first person you need to be true to is yourself, then you can deal with your partner. If you're really not enjoying it, your partner won't either. And if he or she does enjoy it when you're not, you need a new partner.

2. **You're not prepared to deal with the consequences.** No matter how much you'd rather live in a fantasy world of candles, lace,

whipped cream and stilettos, reality WILL intervene. Serious stuff can happen when you have sex, like pregnancy, communicable disease, deeper emotions and expectations. As easily as you sow the seeds of love, you may also be sowing deceit, disappointment or heartache. Can you handle that? Have you really thought it out?

If you're starting a new relationship, whatever the circumstances, are you prepared to deal with the potential outcome, physically and mentally? If the answer is no, you should be saying no. Would you get behind the wheel of your car, steaming drunk, without insurance and no seatbelt? I certainly hope not, which leads me to another point.

3.   **You wouldn't do it sober.** Funny how a few cocktails can make things seem like a good idea – things you wouldn't dream of doing in the cold light of day. If part of your foreplay requires slamming back a couple of drinks (I was going to say stiff ones, but I'm talking about BEFORE, not during), then you ought to change your plans. Be honest. If you need to drug yourself into submission before you'll do something, you probably really don't want to do it anyway.

4.   **You and your partner have different agendas.** One of you is in love. The other, in lust. One of you needs relief from a cold, dead

marriage. The other needs a soul mate. Baby, you're looking for love in all the wrong places. If you're not doing it for the same reasons, you'll end up hurt.

Think of it like sharing a meal together. Generally, you eat when you're hungry – you eat to satisfy a common need. You don't eat to make the other person feel better. You don't think she'll fall in love with you because you shared meatloaf. You don't eat because he wants you to. You eat because you want food. The difference with food is you can each order different entrees. With sex, you're eating off the same plate.

Obviously sharing is important when you're having sex with someone, but I think it's most important that you think of yourself first. Is it something you really want? Don't make love because you think you should, or because the other person wants it, or because you owe them something. Make love because you really want to.

In the best case, sex is a pleasurable physical activity, and ideally, a tangible expression of affection, if not love. In the worst case, it's a duty, a punishment, a disappointment. It is almost always a manifestation of the state of your relationship. If your relationship is good and communication is open, your sex will be good. If your relationship is bad, your sex life will be too.

If you need to say no, it's probably not that you don't like sex, but that you don't like the situation. Don't let anyone make you feel like a prude or "frigid" because you need to say no sometimes. Unless you're a priest (well, hmm, maybe not even then), saying no to sex doesn't mean "no, never," it means "no, not like this." And the only one who can decide that for you is you.

8

AVOID THE
SAME OLD
GRIND

So I was thinking about sex recently – as one does –
not really my own sex, but sex in general. And I was
thinking that I understand why it gets boring in long-
term relationships.

It's not that your partner gets boring, or the sex itself
gets boring. I think it's because the way you VIEW
the sex in your relationship gets boring. And that has
everything to do with how you were taught to view
sex from the very beginning.

From childhood, most of us are taught that anything
to do with sex is "naughty." It's exciting and titillating.
It's hot. It's forbidden. When we see or hear anything
sexy, we giggle or make a face. In our society, sex is
hidden behind a curtain, or in plain brown wrapping.

It's fun and appealing precisely because we're NOT supposed to be doing it!

Every first experience you've had with sex – first kiss, first shag, first time with this or that person, first time in an elevator, first time on a plane, first time in the kosher meat section of the supermarket (ok, maybe not that time, but all the other times...) it was exciting, right? It was exciting because you really weren't supposed to be doing it.

On the other hand, sex on the third Tuesday of the fifth month of the sixth year with your spouse is BORING, because you're thinking I'm SUPPOSED to be doing this. It's no fun if I'm SUPPOSED to be doing it. There's no risk. No frisson of excitement. But why should there be? Why should sex have to be a thrill ride to make it appealing?

I love the feel of a hot shower. I have always loved it. I cannot think of a time (except when I've been ruby red with sunburn) that I have not loved a hot shower. It is a great pleasure to me. It is an essential part of my life. It feels good, and it's never boring. It's a nice hot shower. That's all I want it to be. That's all it has to be. It's a pleasure.

But not sex. It's not a pleasure! It's a little bit scary, and secret and "nasty." And it's no wonder people are disappointed night after night. Their outlook is all wrong!

Let's demystify sex! Take it off the lace, leather and

rubber pedestal. Downgrade it to just another one of life's pleasures, right up there with angora sweaters and new car smell.

A good old squelchy shag. A warm tumble with another naked body. Even if you don't have multiple screaming mutual orgasms, it should at a minimum still be rather nice. And never boring.

How can something pleasurable be boring? Are massages boring? Is chocolate ice cream boring? Is scratching an itch boring? Is a huge, multi-toned belch boring? Never! Because we enjoy most pleasures simply for what they are.

If the sex you're having (and this assumes you ARE having it now and then), isn't a pleasure, before you examine your partner's shortcomings (oops, sorry about the pun) examine the inside of your head. What are your expectations in the first place?

If you still have that notion of illicit, wanton, stolen couplings with cinema-quality lighting, either you are forcing yourself into an ever-escalating search for thrills, or a flatline of disappointment.

And another thing. Don't turn sex into something else entirely. Make sure you're not using sex as a bargaining chip. A debt owed. A conquest. Or a temporary cure for insecurity. How can that be any fun at all? Before you work together with your partner to make your sex life more pleasurable, make certain that's all you want it to be. A pleasure.

9

There's a lot of heartbreak in the world. Or at least, in the part of the world that I talk to. I hear from scores of women with broken hearts who say they just don't understand what happened in their blooming relationships. They meet this nice guy, who pursues them passionately and perhaps even lavishly. They talk on the phone, or email, or date once or twice. And then they have sex.

Sigh.

And then it all changes. He hardly calls. He hardly writes. She wonders what she did wrong. Until the phone rings again.

He calls, they have sex, and she's happy until the

whole cycle starts again. The problem is (and here comes the obvious truth) men and women are different. While she's falling in love, he's falling in lust.

I don't know why it is, it just is. I don't know if it's because men and women truly are different, or we act differently because we're told we're different. I don't know if it has to do with our primeval wiring – that a gazillion years ago male homo sapiens were wired to spread their seed, and females were wired for nurturing. Many scholars wiser than I have built their careers on books about the subject.

But I do know it's not the exception, it's the rule, particularly (and perhaps, unfortunately), in this day and age.

Ladies, let me just put it this way. That guy who's aching to get into your panties an hour, a day or even a week after you met him is most probably NOT looking for the love of his life. If the only place you ever feel you're connecting with him emotionally is between the no-iron percales, you need to do the laundry and send him packing.

It sometimes appears to me that Western society's changed attitude toward sexual activity in the last 40 years has led to more heartbreak in exchange for easy passion.

All the contraceptive precaution in the world is not going to prevent a broken heart. Having said that, hearts were broken before The Pill was invented.

In any case, the easy acceptance we feel for non-, extra- or pre-marital sex means more opportunity for miscommunication and inconsistent expectations, especially when the expectations of men and women are so different to begin with. So let me give you some of my "golden rules:"

1. You're not going to make him love you because you sleep with him.

2. If he only comes back because you have sex with him, you don't want him back.

3. "Making love" doesn't mean he's in love.

4. If he doesn't call you after you finally have sex, you should be happy. He's removed himself from your life. You can move on.

5. If "it all changes" after you have sex, it should give you a big hint. It was never what you thought it was.

And a free bonus (painfully obvious) rule: NEVER I mean NEVER have unprotected sex.

We all have sex for different reasons, at different times in our lives. Of course, the number one reason is to make babies, but that's actually only a very, very small percentage of the time.

To be honest, other than procreation, I think the best reason to have sex is because you simply want to have sex. Not because you want something from your partner, or because you think you should, or because you need love. But because you want good, squelchy sex. I personally believe it is preferable to do it in a mutually loving relationship, but I'm old-fashioned that way.

But it's very, very hard to tell our hearts what to feel. The urge to find love is very, very great. If you have a tendency to fall, ladies (and some gentlemen), don't rush to get naked. And if you do, you must recognize that often one man's lust is another woman's love. Make sure you always know the difference.

10

○ AND THE
DIFFERENCE
BETWEEN LOVE
AND SEX

Here's a brain teaser for you: What's the difference between making love and having sex? Study the following examples.

When making love, you call out your partner's name. When having sex, you try to remember it.

When making love, you talk about it afterwards with your partner. When having sex, you talk about it with your best friend. Sometimes during, if it's that sort of evening.

When making love, you first have a soapy shower, then make love, then go to sleep. When having sex, you have sex, then take a shower, then leave.

When making love, you wear flannel pajamas and socks. When having sex, you wear lace and stilettos (well, the women, primarily).

When making love, the evening probably started in the living room. When having sex, it probably started in the bar.

When making love, it's unusual to be doing it in a car. When having sex, it's unusual to be doing it in a bed.

When having sex, you worry your spouse will find out. When making love, you worry the kids will.

I provide these examples because an acquaintance once took issue with my use of the term "lover" when talking about infidelity in particular. His point was a "lover" is someone you genuinely love, not just lust after. And "making love" is what you do together as an expression of your emotion in a committed relationship. Actually, I agree.

We tend to use the phrase "making love" as a euphemism because we don't like to say "sex" in polite company. But we certainly have plenty of euphemisms for sex: "doing the nasty," " the beast with two backs," "hiding the salami," or "having a shag" spring handily to mind.

However, we really should reserve "making love" for the real thing. We need to remind ourselves that sex is just an "act" – two people acting like they really care about each other, but in reality, they really only care about themselves and their own pleasure.

The problem is, oftentimes one person is working hard at making love, while the other is simply having sex. It's tough, because good sex can be an outcome of good love, but good love generally doesn't spring from good sex. And what makes it even more complicated is our bodies don't know the difference.

I sometimes think we have two brains: upper and lower. The upper brain is responsible for judgment, responsibility and reason. The lower brain is responsible (or should I say irresponsible) for sex. It's the lower brain that gets people into trouble and makes risky behavior seem like a really good idea. The lower brain convinces the upper brain that it really might be love, and the upper brain falls for it. Then when it isn't love, the upper brain gets really cheesed off. But does it blame the lower brain? No! It blames the other person. How stupid is that? If the brains really wanted to know the truth, they'd only need to ask the heart. We always have the right answer in our hearts. We just may not want to hear it.

So perhaps these examples will provide some clarity, and help you understand if it's love or sex. I'll leave you with one more, which is perhaps the most important. When having sex, you're secretly making comparisons. When making love, there is no comparison.

CALLING IT QUITS

1

A friend of mine had been seeing this chap for a few months. She enjoyed his company and was attracted to him, but the "relationship" (such as it was) didn't quite fulfill her needs. He wasn't able to spend as much time with her as she wanted, nor did he seem that keen to "integrate" her into his social circle. However, the time they did share was enjoyable, so she went along with the flow.

Then, late one night and into the wee hours of the morning, they had a long, drawn-out conversation. He told her he wanted to stop seeing her. She was too good for him, and she should move on. He had certain issues he had to deal with and couldn't be in a relationship.

Instead of saying, "You know what? You're right. Thanks for everything. Bye," she tried to convince him he WAS worthy, that they ought to continue (such as it was). She was feeling rejected and needed to feel SHE was worthy.

But she was missing the whole point!! This had nothing to do with her. It was all about HIM.

Has this ever happened to you? You're not in a satisfying relationship. You're not getting what you need out of it, you're not happy, and the other person wants to end it. But you try to convince him (or her) to STAY! What are you, crazy?

This is one time when it's not only okay to be a little a selfish – it's darn near REQUIRED. If you're in an unfulfilling relationship where you're doing most of the giving and the other person is emotionally unavailable, it's not the right relationship for you. He may be wonderful. He may be gorgeous. He may be good with your kids. You may have great sex. But he can't give you all you really need.

It doesn't make him a bad person. Just the wrong person for you. It's like shopping for shoes (isn't everything?). You see a pair of shoes you really like. You try them on. They don't fit, so you don't buy them. You don't get mad at the shoes. You don't get mad at your feet. They're simply not the right shoes for you. You can still appreciate their style and beauty, but you don't take them home.

When you're in a relationship you must always be true to yourself. Check in with yourself often: am I getting what I need? If you're not, you owe it to yourself to tell the other person what you want. Maybe he didn't have any idea.

But maybe he's simply not capable. And that's ok. As long as you don't stay in the relationship – or beg him to stay.

Everyone has a particular way they need to be loved, not what they think they deserve or what they'll accept, what they need. Just like your body has certain requirements to survive, so does your heart. It's up to you to make sure your heart is fully nourished. No one can be responsible for that but you. In a relationship, being with a bad person is not the same as being with the wrong person. The wrong person may be completely lovable, but it doesn't matter if you're not completely loved. Move on.

2

GET OFF YOUR BIG "BUT"

If you're not getting what you want out of your relationship, maybe the problem is your big "but."

As Pee Wee Herman so eloquently put it in "Pee Wee's Big Adventure," "Everybody has a big but." BUT I don't have the time. BUT I'm scared. BUT I don't want to hurt his feelings. Our big buts stop us from fulfilling obligations, trying new things, saying what we feel, and very often, being honest with ourselves. We use our big buts to justify staying in relationships that aren't going anywhere. Let me show you what I mean.

"But I know he really wants to settle down." Exactly what has he done to demonstrate that? By any chance, have you been waiting longer than 12 months for evidence?

"But even though he doesn't act like it, I know he's caring and sensitive." Really? How? By the way he treats the dog?

"But I know she'd like me, if she got to know me." Hmm. Do you ever actually speak to her beyond hello?

"But he can be so affectionate and warm." Let me guess – it's generally either after a few beers, after he hasn't been with you for a few weeks, or after midnight.

"But she promised me she's going to change." And she's said that how many times?

"But other than that, we have a great relationship."

The point is: are you using your but to justify your efforts in keeping an unfulfilling, unsatisfying relationship alive? If you must counter the facts as they present themselves with a "but," you're no longer thinking with your head, you're thinking with your but.

What you hope should not be confused with what is. Make sure you're not falling in love with the dream, but the reality. I fear many relationships and marriages are founded on beautiful dreams, which may not even be shared by both partners! No wonder there's disappointment down the road. They fell in love with the potential, what they hoped he or she would become. When it doesn't happen, they get upset because the other person "failed." They failed to make the dream come true.

It's always much nicer to fall in love with a dream than reality. Dreams are perfect, softly-lit with a flattering bulb, wrinkle-free. Reality is messy, smelly and a lot of times, not very fun. But it's genuine, truthful, and sincere.

Don't let your "but" dreams convince you to stick around in dead-end relationships. Sometimes it's hard for us to admit we've made a mistake, or a misjudgment. We just hate to admit we were wrong about someone – particularly if our friends or family "told us so." Gosh-darn it! I'll prove them wrong. I'll grit my teeth and stick with this. Well, you deserve better. And you certainly don't need to punish yourself by throwing more of your precious time after a bad decision. It's time to get off your but!

3

ARE YOU A DOORMAT?

Can you believe what this woman once told me:

"My husband has to have at least three women at his disposal at any given time of his life. He makes them fall in love with him by doing all the right things a woman would want from a man. Once in his system, he moves to the next and so on. When one woman gets wiser or fed up and decides to move on, he too moves to the next victim. This has been his lifestyle. He believes God brought him to this world with a purpose, to procreate. Yes some of those women who were weak and succumbed to his lies and believed he would marry them actually have children by him and of course that was another reason for losing interest, 'forcing him' or using childbearing as 'pressure' to marry. What is he, a sex addict? Pure and simple womanizer, liar, or is he psycho??"

Well, of course my reply was, "Forget the husband, what the heck is the WIFE?" (or words to that effect).

Sure, it's natural to wonder what kind of a man would do these things. What kind of a man would be so selfish, so irresponsible, so amoral? But SHEESH who cares? What I want to know is what kind of a woman puts up with this crap?

Ladies, the holiday season will eventually roll around. Give yourself a present. Buy a new doormat, so you can stop being one.

There's absolutely no excuse for standing by and watching this behavior, and worse, just letting it go on without doing anything about it. This man has no respect for you, your kids, the other women or your marriage "vows." It's a joke!

Having said that, you need to understand what is making him do this. So ask him and see if you can get some semblance of reason out of him. There's an outside chance it's something in your relationship that needs to be fixed. After all, with a lot of communication and working together, a relationship can recover from one infidelity. Theoretically.

But CONSTANT messing around? There's a serious problem here. This man doesn't want to be a husband, a committed provider, he wants to be at a buffet. All-you-can-eat. And the ridiculous thing is there are plenty of women willing to line up as dish of the day.

Gals, WHAT are you thinking? You think you can change him? That it'll be different with you? Think again, honey.

If you stay with him, you are enabling him. You make that behavior possible. He's messing around with a million different women, because you let him. Sorry, but it's true.

Kick him out. Break up with him. Divorce him. And forget about trying to change him. Change YOURSELF. Figure out what it is that attracts you to someone like him. What is it deep inside that allows you to accept a man like this and his unacceptable behavior? Because I'll bet it's not the first time. But you can make it the last.

4

○ WOULD YOU
PLEASE LISTEN
TO YOURSELF?

We always complain that our partners don't listen to us when we tell them how we feel, but let me ask you a question. Do you actually listen to YOURSELF?

I am amazed, simply amazed at the emails I get. I am very honored that so many people are willing to share their relationship issues with me, but there are so many at whom I'd like to shout "WHAT THE HECK ARE YOU THINKING???"

I get bunches of emails that start out something like, "I've got this boyfriend I've been seeing for X months and it started out with great sex blah blah blah and now after awhile I'm not sure how he feels about me blah blah blah," and then buried in another paragraph somewhere "by the way we're both married to other people."

AAAAAck! How can I be the only one who sees something wrong with this picture!!

Or another typical email: "I really love my partner, but lately I'm not sure he's right for me blah blah blah he hasn't been as attentive, and of course I support both of us and our 3 year old because he's unemployed blah blah blah and I had to make him move out a month ago because he was drinking and physically abusive. Should I take him back?"

What??

When people send these emails, are they not reading their own words? Perhaps I'm being insensitive. Taking the time to write and ask for advice is an important first step, and if I can help be the catalyst to get someone out of a dangerous or unhealthy relationship, I am truly thankful.

But still! When you write down your thoughts about your relationship, and what's bothering you, READ WHAT YOU'VE WRITTEN. Look at what you're saying. The key to the problem may well be in front of your nose, the solution staring at you, if only you'll stare back.
Maybe I can make it easier for you. I've developed a little "emotional spell check" guide you can apply to what you write. Here is a selection of common phrases.

Sex is great with my boyfriend, but I love my husband. Yeah right. Sort out the issues with your marriage. Fix it, or end it. Then you can think about a boyfriend.

We live XX hours/XXX miles apart and he's only visited once. This man needs to show some initiative. It needs to go both ways.

He says it's all my problem/all in my head and won't talk about it. Then maybe he'd like to talk about breaking up? If you can't talk about issues together, try counseling. If he won't go with you, go alone.

All he wants to do is look at porn. If it's every single day, it's not normal. Get him into counseling, or get him out the door.

Even though he never calls, I can't let him go. What do you mean? He's already gone. It's over. Move on.

We're both 17 and love each other, but now I'm not sure about marriage. At 17, you shouldn't be. Take some time to get to know YOURSELF as an adult before you make a commitment.

He says it's not just the sex and he loves me, but we never go out. Oh please. It's all about the sex. If you need more than that, you need someone else.

I'm living with my parents right now because of money issues and it's putting pressure on my relationship. And this surprises you? Your first priority should be sorting yourself out and securing your independence. THEN you can think about a relationship.

He says he loves me but can't leave his wife right now. Oh, and this is the very first time in history someone has said this. It means he'd rather be with her. No matter how much he enjoys you, he's not willing to make the trade-off.

I hope this little list helps get you started. It's incredible how we manage to complicate our lives because we miss the simplest solutions. You really DO have the power to change your situation, break bad habits and avoid heartache. But the first person you need to listen to is yourself.

5

DON'T MAKE
THE MISTAKE
OF NOT FIXING
YOUR MISTAKE

Everyone makes mistakes. Everyone! It's just part of life. In fact, at the risk of being too morbid, I can quite confidently say the only people who don't mistakes are dead ones.

So if you're alive (and I know you are, because you're reading this), you have already made a mistake, or you're on the verge of making one. I don't know what it is, but I know it's out there, looming in your future. And chances are one or more of the mistakes looming out there (or hanging over you right now) bears an amazing resemblance to your husband, wife, boyfriend or girlfriend. Am I right, or am I right?

Yep, you made a mistake. Despite all the red flags,

warnings and bad gut feelings, you decided to trust the wrong person. Or love the wrong person. Or marry the wrong person. Or have a baby with the wrong person. You blew it.

So NOW what do you do? How are you gonna get out of this one? Well, in the midst of your angst, there is good news. There is ALWAYS a way forward. You may not like it. It may not be easy. But there is always a way to correct mistakes. Even in relationships.

To help you on your way, I have devised this handy guide for correcting relationship mistakes.

1.   **First of all, admit you made a mistake.** Making a mistake is not such a bad thing. But failing to recognize it IS. We learn through mistakes. They may be harsh teachers, but sometimes they are the only lessons we remember. However, you will never learn from a mistake if you don't recognize it and acknowledge you made it in the first place. Take responsibility for your actions. Admit you made a boo-boo. Make sure you understand completely (and I do mean completely) how and why you got yourself into this situation in the first place. What signs did you ignore? What dreams did you mistake for reality? What habits do you need to change? Write it all down and study it carefully. You will need this information the next time around.

2.   **Now immediately forgive yourself.** This is critical. You will be unable to move forward if you do not let go of the past. Stop beating yourself up. You did it. It's over. Now do everything in your power to make sure it doesn't happen again.

3.   **Speak up.** So you realize you're with the wrong person, or they're not treating you right. SAY something. You are not powerless in a relationship. You always have the power to say, "This is not working for me." You have the power to get help. You cannot change how people react to you, but you CAN change how you react to them. Staying silent will not fix a mistake. It creates a new one. But speaking up and demanding action may provide a solution.

4.   **Accept change.** If you made a relationship mistake, things will have to change. But my gawd, don't you want them to? Things suck right now! Why are you afraid of leaving that? If you say there are too many things you cannot give up, then perhaps it wasn't a mistake after all. If you can't give up the life you have now, that is YOUR choice. And you will have to live with the consequences, good and bad.

5.   **Make a decision.** The only bad decision is no decision. You may make a decision to do nothing about the situation (see above), but that is still a decision. Mistakes generally don't

simply go away, like pimples. They continue to grow and affect the future. Every minute you spend doing nothing after making a mistake makes the mistake even bigger. Once that minute is passed, it's gone forever. That's your life ticking away. Your whole life does not need to be a mistake. Do something about it. Do not pay for your mistake with your life.

Making a mistake is easy. If it weren't so easy, we wouldn't do it so often. Whims, passions, fantasies, insecurities, piña coladas...all make mistakes happen. It may seem unfair that fixing them is so difficult. But it is. That's just the way it goes. The only way to make it easier is never make a mistake in the first place. But that's difficult. In life, you will make mistakes. Don't make the mistake of not fixing them.

6

○ "GIVE AND
TAKE" DOESN'T
MEAN YOU GIVE
AND HE TAKES

Can you please help me with something? I don't
understand these emails I've received:

"My boyfriend has been out of work for over year. He
lives with me and our son, but he hasn't tried to find a
job for months. I'm working to support all of us. My
boyfriend goes out a lot on weekends, and
sometimes doesn't come home until the next day. But
the thing is, I really love him."

Excuse me?

Or how about this one: "I've been married 14 years to
my husband and it's like I don't exist. At night when
he comes home, he hardly talks to me, just watches
TV. We never go out, and I think the last time we had

sex was 6 months ago. If I ever try to talk to him about it he just gets angry at me. But I love him completely and can't imagine living without him."

Well, yeah, I suppose after 14 years of that it WOULD be hard to imagine not being miserable.

But am I missing something here? What definition of "love" are these women using?

Now I know there are many different types of love. There's the love you feel for your children. The love you feel for your pet, or your best friend. I have many pairs of shoes I absolutely love. I LOVE getting a massage. But the love I feel for my partner is something completely different.

I respect and admire him as a person. I enjoy being with him, and of course I find him very attractive. But I also get a lot in return. He cares about me, listens to my problems and shares the load of life. I love him for that.

Call me selfish, but I think part of the definition of romantic love is getting something back. I couldn't love someone or want to stay in a relationship with someone if it was only a one-way exchange. I might admire and respect him as a person, but I certainly couldn't be IN love.

The ladies in these emails may share many years of experience with these men. They may even care about them and respect them as people (although based on what they say, I can't imagine why). But saying they LOVE these men?

I think it's the IDEA of love they love. The idea of having a husband or partner. The idea of the father of your child. The idea of a life-long companion.

When I hear these stories from people who say they love their partners, despite how poorly they're being treated, I don't hear love, I hear fear. Fear of being alone. As long as they can keep telling themselves they love these losers, they can convince themselves they're in a relationship – albeit one way.

A partner, boyfriend, girlfriend, husband or wife who doesn't respect you, care about you or treat you with love, doesn't deserve yours. There's no point in loving 'em if they won't love you back.

7

○ STOP HOLDING
ON TO A
FANTASY

How many good days, months, even years have you wasted holding on to "love?" I've done my share of it. And I know you have, because I read the emails. So why do we do it?

We do it because where love is concerned – and particularly bad love – we have a very screwy sense of time and reality. Although we are LIVING in the here and now, we are LOVING either in the past or in the future.

First, let's agree on your here and now, your reality. I'm not talking about the so-called "reality" we see on television. I'm talking about your own personal reality. The reality you're experiencing today, this minute.

Your reality right this minute is sitting and reading this. You're doing it in a certain place, wearing certain clothes. At this moment in time, your health has a particular condition, your hair is one way or another, you're at work or at home, maybe drinking coffee. It's night or day, rainy or clear. That's your reality.

There's another reality as well – the one dealing with your relationship. This instant, this very instant, when you think of your partner/lover/spouse, what is your reality? Happy? Sad? Frustrated? Fulfilled? Disappointed? This is also your reality. Now. It is not the past. It is not the future. It is now.

So when you say you love your current partner/lover/spouse, exactly what moment in time are you talking about? Can you say you love that person for the way he or she is at this moment? For the way you are being treated at this moment in time? For the way she makes you feel at this instant?

At this time in your relationship, is your partner being honest and loving? Is he demonstrating by his word and action that you are a priority, that he cares about you and wants to be with you or work with you to make things better? No matter how you answer these questions, this is your reality.

If you answered "yes" to most of the above, you love your reality. It doesn't matter what the past was or what the future holds. You're living and loving the same thing.

However.

If you answered "no" a lot, it's a different story. If you answered "no" a lot, and you still tell me you love him, what exactly are you loving? I think it's either one of two things.

You're either loving the past you once had, or the future you HOPE you will. But that's a whole lot different than loving the PERSON right now.

You may love what happened in the past and remember fondly what happened then. But you cannot live there now. It's gone. Done. Over. No matter how great it was, it's not what's happening now. There is no point in holding on to love because of what once was. No matter how great it was (or seemed like it was), what only matters now is what IS. You cannot go back. You can only go forward.

But you can only go forward so far. I don't know about you, but I'm not very good at foretelling the future. I can make some pretty good guesses about tomorrow, maybe as far as next week, but that's about it. Okay, in a stretch, maybe even a month from now, but beyond that, forget it. Beyond that, I'm just making it up. I'm hoping.

If you keep holding on to love for someone because you're hoping maybe, just maybe, the future might be a little different and everything will change and you'll get what you want, I think you're making a mistake.

If you're hoping your lover may change, or say the magic words, or turn back into the person you first met, despite the fact that there is nothing in his current behavior or words to indicate he's interested in doing any of that, exactly what do you think is going to happen to make it happen? A voodoo spell? A genie?

I'm not saying you should always ditch your relationship if it's not what you want right this minute. People have moods and go through good and bad patches. But if the person you're with is not committed to you here and now, not committed to working with you today and the next, he or she is not worthy of your love, no matter what happened in the past, or what you hope for the future.

8

"STUFF" IS NOT A REASON TO STAY

I once got an email from a woman who had all the right "stuff" in her marriage, but after many years in this union was deeply unhappy, to the point of despair. How could this be? With all this stuff, there must be love there somewhere (just as the young boy said when confronted with a pile of manure, "There must be a pony in here.") She and her husband had a nice home, cars, income.

But the key is none of these things had anything to do with love. They're just things.

It often seems we want to get into relationships for love, but end up staying because of "stuff." Stuff is how we measure our success. Stuff is how others judge us. We get so attached to our stuff, we are willing to put up with misery and pain. We are willing to trade our happiness just to hold on to the stuff. In fact, we're paying for it with our lives.

Are you really willing to trade your soul for a duplex?

Look, I know it's not that simple. I know (from experience) when you're entwined financially in a relationship it's very hard to unravel. It's taken you years to set up the household, the routine, the utilities. But is the tv and stereo really more valuable than the fulfillment of your own life? Do you really want to make a dining room set the battleground for your frustration?

I know starting all over again is expensive and time consuming. I've been there. I had some really cool stuff, and now I don't anymore. But now I have other stuff. And most importantly, I have my happiness and peace of mind.

After I left the 3 bedroom house, filled with designer Italian furniture and a stereo the price of a small car, and moved into a little apartment with a futon and cushions on the floor, I couldn't have been happier. I did a little dance. I had less of everything, except contentment.And that was worth everything to me.

If you stay in a relationship because you're afraid of losing the "stuff," you're making a very bad trade.

If I've said it once, I've said it 4,978,543 times (or thereabouts), everything in life is a trade-off. Stay in an unhappy relationship because of the stuff, and you'll have things but no happiness. Leave the relationship and the stuff for happiness, and accept you might have an uphill slog to get everything back. The decision is yours. The life is yours.

There is ALWAYS an alternative, always a choice you can make. Of course we'd like it to be easy and painless, but it probably won't be. There is generally always a cost associated with change, one way or another. But what is that compared to the cost of a life stuck in the molasses of misery?

I just think life is too short to spend unhappy. How productive can you be, how much love can you give to your friends or children if you're miserable yourself?

As far as I know, we only get one go-round on this planet. Don't waste another day. Show the world what stuff you're made of.

9

YOU CAN'T SWITCH TO "JUST FRIENDS"

So a guy named Mike B shared a disturbing story with me. Disturbing, because I've heard it so many times before, and familiar, because I probably lived a version of it myself once or twice. So here's our buddy Mike, in a pretty serious relationship for the past three years, and all of a sudden his girl wants to break up with him, but here's the kicker- she still wants to be FRIENDS.

What the heck is THAT supposed to mean? I can completely understand poor Mike's anguish. I mean, perhaps over time one's feelings can morph from one thing into another, but you simply can't turn your feelings on and off like a light switch. Today, passionate love. Tomorrow, click! Just your buddy, tell me ALL about the new guy you're dating. Yeah, right.

What are we thinking when we say something like that? I think we do it because we think it will lessen the pain. I'm going to slide out of your life slowly rather than yank myself out in one go. Or there are lots of things I like about you, but not quite enough to actually want to be your girlfriend/boyfriend. Can I just have the parts I like?

There are very rare situations where two people decide together that perhaps a platonic arrangement is better than a romantic one, and there are definitely situations where the romantic relationship turns into a platonic one over time (although generally it's not a conscious decision).

But to think the other person can simply switch overnight is not only impossible, but selfish. Because I'm pretty darn sure Mike B's girlfriend has been thinking about being "just friends" for some time. She only sprung it on him now. The signs have probably been there, and perhaps Mike missed them. It may be their relationship already started drifting in the platonic direction, but he hadn't noticed. For although we often expect the other person to change overnight in order to catch up, we've had the "luxury" of weeks, months or even years of slow percolation to get where we are.

However, there is one thing I want to make clear. I'm not saying that Mike B is totally blameless in the break-up. He might be, or he might not be. I don't know anything about the circumstances or why his girlfriend's feelings changed.

All I'm saying is it's pretty unreasonable for her to expect to him to be able – let alone WANT – to be "just friends." She's breaking up with him, pure and simple. If she doesn't want to be with him, she doesn't want to be with him. And that's the end of it.

Sorry Mike, but that's the way I see it. Sadly, it's time to move on. When the pain is gone, and the wounds have healed, it may be possible to resume a casual friendship with her. But that's not something you are required to "try" for. It happens on its own accord. And it's rare. For now, it's time for introspection and time on your own to reflect on how things got to this point, and then you'll be ready to move on. Sigh.

10

◯ YAY, IT'S OVER

A few pages back, I wrote about the little smoke signals your brain sends when your relationship begins to ever so slightly crumble around the edges. Based on the emails I receive, many of you are familiar with the signs. And there are many of you for whom it seems the signs don't point to something beginning, but are more indicative of The End, which is sad. Or is it?

Being in a healthy, balanced, committed relationship is one of life's most fulfilling experiences. Being in a relationship which is not is torture.

It's sad that the relationship can't provide the happiness and fulfillment we were looking for when we entered into it. It's sad that once we're in a broken relationship we're not able to fix it – especially when the relationship involves children.

But when you're finally able to break free from a relationship that was causing you stress, pain and heartache, sapping the very essence of your life's energy out of you, it's not sad, it's GREAT! It's like someone has stopped hitting your head with a hammer. The blisters on your feet have disappeared. The ten thousand pound weight is off your shoulders. But sad? Are you kidding?

Actually, I'll tell you why we grieve when a relationship ends, what really makes us sad. We're mourning the loss of the DREAM. The dream of happily ever after, endless passionate love during which no one ever makes a squelchy sound, self-fulfillment, feeling beautiful or handsome, and 2.1 adorable kids.

The dream makes us stay in relationships that are way past their sell-by date. It's the dream that got us into the relationship in the first place. It's the dream that makes one perfect evening surrounded by three frustrating weeks seem like a guarantee of eternal bliss.

But it's not the reality. The reality, in reality, sucked. The reality was no communication, no honesty, and no give and take. The reality was infidelity, incompatibility and dissatisfaction. And you're sad to give that up? I don't think so.

When it's time to end a relationship, you must remind yourself over and over that it's ending because of the cold, hard reality. It's sad your dream is gone, but it never came true in the first place. Let it go. Forgive yourself for making mistakes. And then move on.

But don't forget what it's like to see the difference between the dream and the reality. Because you'll definitely need that skill when the next relationship comes along.

11

THE ART OF
LETTING GO

You know, I don't think the other half in our
relationships can ever torture us as much as we
torture ourselves. No matter how emotionally cruel he
was, how coldly she dropped you, or how painfully
long and drawn-out the break-up process was during
the endless stream of his creative excuses and
watery promises, you'll probably still do a more
thorough job of beating yourself up.

Because you just can't let go.

Why do we do this? Why do we put a death-grip on
something we should drop like a radioactive hot
potato? Why do we cling to fruitless hopes? We're
only prolonging the agony and preventing ourselves
from moving forward, out of the miserable gloom and

into the bright, cheery sunshine where fuzzy squirrels frolic and birdies twitter.

Because it's hard.

Well I'd like to provide some handy instructions on how to let go. A few simple steps to help you quickly get out of the dark and into the light once again.

Focus on the reality, not the dream.
The primary reason we can't let go is because we can't let go of The Dream. What might have been. What could be. The Dream is a very powerful force. The Dream gets us together with someone in the first place, keeps us there, and makes it very hard to leave.

The Dream helps us ignore shortcomings and disappointments because it hovers out there in the future always slightly out of reach, but always beckoning. It's the most seductive, wonderful image, because you conjure it up perfectly to match your desires.

But when your relationship ends, you must remind yourself that The Dream is actually The Pile of Crap. Your relationship is ending because of The Reality - which truly sucked, my friends, or you wouldn't be ending it, would you! So when you're sitting there, crying into your tub of super fudge crunch ribbon, focus on the reality and how relieved you are to be rid of it.

Allow yourself to get mad.
Once you get a good picture of the reality in your head, you will most likely be a little peeved. This is a good thing. Be mad as hell. Be angry that you wasted so much time (and probably money) on this loser. It's okay to be mad. You're hurt! You're disappointed! And it wasn't just your fault. This person cheated, or lied, or didn't hold up his side of the bargain. You just blew a whole bunch of love and time and energy on someone who didn't deserve it. I'd be mad too.

Allow yourself to get mad at yourself.
Face it, you made a mistake. Maybe there was no way you could have known it would end up this way, but between you and me, I doubt it. We do such a good job of ignoring warning signs at the outset (because of The Dream, see above). But when you look back at how you got into this mess, most likely you'll see things now you should have seen then. It's frustrating, and you feel like a sucker, but it happened. Sometimes we get mad at other people instead of getting mad at ourselves. But you need to step up to the plate and admit you made a boo-boo. Get mad at yourself. Accept responsibility for your actions, and then stop beating yourself up. The most valuable thing you can take from the experience is the lesson of how not to do it again.

Spill your guts.
You need to be able to let out your anger, hurt and frustration, and ideally you want to be able to tell the other person how terrible he's making you feel right to his face. But often it's not practical – or

appropriate. Which is not to say it's impossible. You will be amazed how much better you'll feel if you bang out all your pain in a letter. Leave no stone of anger unturned! Pile on the vitriol! Vent your spleen to your heart's (spleen's?) content. And then put the letter in a drawer. The simple act of venting is as good as venting in person.

Change your routine.
The last step in your process of letting go is actually your first step forward. Start doing things differently. Everything you do "the way you used to do it" pulls you back. Make up a new routine just for you. Rearrange the furniture. Find a new restaurant. Have a massage every Friday after work. Throw away the "we" stuff and buy some more "me" stuff.

It's not going to be quick or easy. The old adage that time is the great healer is true. We're all very accustomed to instant gratification, but when it comes to letting go, the only thing we can do instantly is make an effort. You must proactively and patiently build your new life. What's holding you back from moving forward? You are. Remember, you can't grab something new and wonderful unless your hands are free. You must let go.

12

BEING ALONE CAN BE A BEAUTIFUL THING

I get a lot of emails from men, especially young ones for some reason, who are very concerned about finding someone to be in a relationship with. Like it's almost desperation. Like your life is over if you can't find someone to call your own.

First of all, let me tell you we gals can smell desperation a mile away. The more anxious you are, the faster we'll run screaming in the opposite direction. (Of course it goes for us too. If we're desperate to be in a relationship, you sense it and do the same thing, right?)

But the larger issue is this. Instead of trying to mask your desperation and appear cool, how about not being desperate in the first place? I know that human (if not animal) nature gives us the "urge to merge" and life is indeed better with someone to share it. But it can be wonderful on your own. And should be.

In fact, in my opinion, you should not even attempt a relationship UNTIL you're comfortable being on your own. The desperation probably comes because you're not.

Being on your own can be a wonderful thing when you are comfortable with yourself. You can do all your favorite things. You don't have to keep the conversation going. You never have to worry about saying something stupid. You can be completely selfish in your thoughts and your actions. You won't be upset if you don't call yourself back when you said you would. You can make rude noises and eat bad food.

And most importantly, when you spend time on your own, you can get to know yourself and find out exactly how to make yourself happy. One thing I feel very strongly about is that we must be responsible for our own happiness.

Once you are content on your own and know how to make yourself happy, you'll be able to welcome someone else into your life to enhance it. Finding someone will NOT make you happy. It may make you happy-ER, but it will not make you happy. After all, if YOU don't know what makes you happy, how can you possibly expect some stranger to know? And then the worst thing you can possibly do is blame that poor unsuspecting person for not making you happy. It's so unfair! Remember, the other person is in your life to enhance your happiness and contentment. You have to find your own happiness first.

And the most magical thing happens when you are content and happy with yourself. Other people notice. They are attracted to you and want to be with you. The very best advertising you can do to find a partner is to not NEED one. Want is different than need.

Figure out how to love yourself and who you are, be content in your own company and know how to make yourself happy. Stop needing someone, and you will find the person you want.

Made in the USA
Lexington, KY
25 May 2010